★
ICONS

Cover:
Frigidaire, 1965
Endpapers:
Motorola, 1962
Page 1:
Smirnoff, 1966

Steven Heller is the author and editor of over 80 books on graphic design and popular culture, including *Design Literacy: Understanding Graphic Design*, *The Graphic Design Reader*, *Graphic Style: From Victorian to Digital*, and *Counter Culture: The Allure of Mini-Mannequins*.

To stay informed about upcoming TASCHEN titles, please request our magazine at www.taschen.com or write to TASCHEN, Hohenzollernring 53, D–50672 Cologne, Germany, Fax: +49-221-254919. We will be happy to send you a free copy of our magazine which is filled with information about all of our books.

© 2003 TASCHEN GmbH
Hohenzollernring 53, D–50672 Köln
www.taschen.com

Editor: Jim Heimann, Los Angeles
Layout: Claudia Frey, Cologne
Cover Design: Claudia Frey and Angelika Taschen, Cologne
Production: Tina Ciborowius, Cologne
Editorial coordination: Sonja Altmeppen, Cologne
German translation: Sebastian Viebahn, Cologne
French translation: Simone Manceau, Paris
Spanish translation: Gemma Deza Guil for LocTeam, S. L., Barcelona
Japanese translation: Mari Kiyomiya, Chiba

Printed in Italy
ISBN 3–8228–2402–X
ISBN 4–88783–195–1 (edition with Japanese cover)

ALL-AMERICAN ADS
60^S

Ed. Jim Heimann

TASCHEN

KÖLN LONDON LOS ANGELES MADRID PARIS TOKYO

Advertising in the Sixties:

So, What's the Big Idea?

by Steven Heller

If the advertisements in this volume were the sole artifacts a historian used to examine and analyze the turbulent sixties, a picture of American culture would emerge that bears scant resemblance to social and political realities of the times. Where are the Blacks, Latinos, or Asians? Viewed from this vantage point, the sixties had no civil rights movement, Vietnam War, or sex, drugs, and rock and roll. The advertisements here, exhumed from the crypts of Madison Avenue as mummified in the mass magazines of the day, were sanitized, homogenized, and cauterized, which is not to say that they did not have style, taste, or humor, or that they do not represent the zeitgeist in a jaundiced way.

Advertising at this time was designed to out-smart, out-do, and out-sell competition, through whatever means tolerable within the parameters of "truth in advertising" doctrines — which is a concept akin to allowing acceptable amounts of rat hair in food. What's more, by the early sixties postwar Americans were happily conditioned to believe anything that the mass media put forth, and advertising was embraced without question or hesitation, viewed even as entertainment. During the sixties, advertising evolved from its primordial emphasis on lengthy, turgid texts to snappy, witty headlines and picture ensembles through a method known as the "Big Idea." The term connotes both a radical shift from the past and a distinctly American genre of creative promotion. The pioneers of the "Creative Revolution" realized that to truly capture an audience's attention and impart lasting messages they had to continually amuse. So to keep the public on their feet Mad Ave had to call in some of its biggest creative guns.

The gun is an apt metaphor because an advertising campaign is no different from a battlefield maneuver. The larger the artillery or the better the strategy or the greater the manpower, the more hearts and minds will be won over. Continual bombardment of slogans and images clearly reduced resistance and built recognition. If the product being advertised actually lived up to the claims, so much the better. But this was not even necessary if the battle was uncontested. Witness the advertisements for some of the sixties' leading brands — Maidenform, Anacin®, General Electric, and Clairol®. While the products efficiently did their jobs, in each case their fake mythologies gave them a stature and sales appeal that commanded a strong market share, until eventually they were challenged by an even more formidable competitor. Fortunes of existing products were often changed through smarter, if also more relentless, advertising campaigns, and new brands earned affluence through what in the Madison Avenue argot is known as spectacular "creative."

During the sixties, the Big Idea made advertising decidedly cleverer, funnier, and more enjoyable than ever before. New standards were set by the wunderkinder of Madison Avenue, such as art directors George Lois, Gene Federico, Bill Taubin, Helmut Krone, Bob Gage and others, who captured the power inherent in good typography and strong imagery, thereby adding touches of class to ads that did not turn noses up at the masses but afforded them greater respect. Yet their respective gems were set alongside many cheaper stones. The sixties was a transitory period in which the Creative Revolution fought the mediocre status quo. An early sixties ad for the soft drink Dr Pepper®, which sought to siphon market share away from Coke® and Pepsi®, for example, shows a thirsty lass dreaming of another Pepper, in what was little more than a costly exercise for the advertising agency. Yet an ad for 7 UP® used a much more unconventional, expressive approach: Rather than a photograph or realistic painting, the bold step of using a conceptual illustration of a man watching a football game (seen in the lens of his binoculars), with barely a hint of the bottle (it was convention in all such ads to show the product), gave the viewer an added message to ponder. Now that was gutsy. Slowly mass-market advertisements were injected with more original attributes.

The sixties gave birth to its classics with crafty headlines and taglines designed to wheedle into the mass subconscious. Many were innocuous, others insipid. Of the latter, cigarette slogans were often the most memorable, including one for Lucky Strike® Filters that went "Show Me a Filter Cigarette That Really Delivers and I'll Eat My Hat!" While the verbiage may seem unwieldy, it was unforgettable when wed to a photograph of an attractive model whose hat has a large bite chomped out of it. One ad in this lengthy campaign shows a Vietnamese woman sheepishly smiling under her traditional straw head-gear in perhaps one of the few tips of the hat, so to speak, to America's geopolitical involvement in Southeast Asia (as a dumping ground for cigarettes, among other things). Certain advertisements are considered classics because they somehow promoted a lifestyle that became an integral part of the zeitgeist. Clairol's ads, for example, made it socially imperative for every woman to change her hair color, and the slogan "Does She Or Doesn't She, Only Her Hairdresser Knows for Sure," under-scored how easy and effective it was.

Advertising will never be neutral. It must always demonstrate that one thing is better than the next thing, and that that thing is also the best thing. During the sixties the definition of hard-sell changed from bang-the-consumer-over-the-head with trite words and pictures to creative playfulness presum-ably geared to make the receiver feel better about advertising. And it worked. But regardless of method, the advertisements in this volume — truly the backbone of a market-driven capitalist economy — are guided by one simple agenda: To build such incomparable recognition that the public will clamor, desire, and demand whatever is being sold to them. And that in a nutshell is the Big Idea.

Werben in den Sechzigern:

Auf der Suche nach der „Big Idea"

von Steven Heller

Wenn die Werbung in diesem Band das einzige Quellenmaterial wäre, auf das sich ein Historiker bei seiner Analyse der sechziger Jahre stützen könnte, würde ein Bild von der amerikanischen Gesellschaft entstehen, das mit der sozialen und politischen Realität jener Zeit nur eine entfernte Ähnlichkeit hätte. Wo sind die Schwarzen, die Latinos oder Asiaten? Die Werbung nahm keine Notiz von Bürgerrechtsbewegung, Vietnamkrieg, Sex and Drugs and Rock 'n' Roll. Was sich gleichsam mumifiziert in den verstaubten Archiven der großen Werbeagenturen an der New Yorker Madison Avenue erhalten hat, war immer schon steril. Was nicht heißt, dass es den Anzeigen an Stil, Geschmack oder Humor gefehlt hätte oder sie nicht dem Zeitgeist entsprochen hätten.

Die Werbung dieser Zeit legte es darauf an, die Konkurrenz auszustechen und auszutricksen – auf allen Gebieten und mit allen Mitteln, die nach dem „Truth-in-Advertising"-Gesetz gerade noch zulässig waren; dessen Bestimmungen gegen den irreführenden und unlauteren Wettbewerb könnte man mit Vorschriften über eine zulässige Höchstmenge für Rattenhaar in Lebensmitteln vergleichen. Außerdem glaubten die Amerikaner in den frühen Sechzigern so bereitwillig alles, was die Massenmedien verkündeten, dass sie auch die Werbung bedenkenlos konsumierten, sie gar als Unterhaltung betrachteten. In den Sechzigern entwickelte sich die Werbung weg von langen Texten hin zu stärkeren Bildern mit spritzigen Headlines. Ganz so, wie es das „Big Idea"-Konzept forderte. Es brach mit den Strategien der Vergangenheit und führte zum originär amerikanischen Genre der kreativen Werbung. Die Pioniere der „Creative Revolution" hatten entdeckt, dass sie ihr Publikum stets von neuem unterhalten mussten, um seine Aufmerksamkeit zu fesseln und eigene Aussagen nachhaltiger vermitteln zu können. Dazu musste die Madison Ave schweres kreatives Geschütz auffahren.

„Geschütz" ist hier eine passende Metapher, weil sich eine Werbekampagne in nichts von einem militärischen Feldzug unterscheidet: Je schlagkräftiger die Artillerie, je besser die Strategie oder je größer die Truppenstärke, desto mehr Herzen und Hirne lassen sich erobern. Ein anhaltendes Bombardement mit Slogans und Bildern zermürbt spürbar die Widerstandskraft und erhöht den Wiedererkennungswert. Wenn das beworbene Produkt den behaupteten Eigenschaften auch entsprach – umso besser. Unbedingt notwendig war es nicht, denn nicht immer gab es echte Gegner. Genannt seien hier die Kampagnen für einige der in den Sechzigern führenden Marken: Maidenform, Anacin®, General Electric und Clairol®. Die Produkte erfüllten nicht nur einfach ihren Zweck. Der geborgte Mythos verlieh ihnen Status und „Sales-Appeal", so dass sie alle große Marktanteile hielten. Anders, wenn ein beeindruckenderer Gegner sie herausforderte: Neue Marken gewannen Zulauf durch spektakuläre „creatives", wie solche Kampagnen im Jargon der Madison Ave heißen.

Infolge des „Big Idea"-Prinzips war die Werbung in den Sechzigern pfiffiger, lustiger und unterhaltsamer als je zuvor. Die Wunderkinder der Madison Ave – Artdirectors wie George Lois, Gene Federico, Bill Taubin, Helmut Krone, Bob

Gage, die die Macht einer guten Typografie und einer intensiven Bildsprache erkannt hatten – setzten neue Maßstäbe. Sie kreierten Anzeigen, die auf eine elitäre Abgrenzung verzichteten und setzten seltene Glanzlichter im grauen Gesamtszenario, denn noch kämpfte die „Creative Revolution" gegen das vorherrschende Mittelmaß an. Eine Anzeige für den Softdrink Dr Pepper® z. B. war für die Werbeagentur kaum mehr als eine kostspielige Fingerübung: Um den Konkurrenten Coke® und Pepsi® das Wasser abzugraben, ließen sie ein Mädchen von einem weiteren Pepper-Drink träumen. Einen unkonventionelleren Weg ging 7 UP®. Statt auf eine Fotografie oder ein realistisches Gemälde zu setzen, zeigte man nur schemenhaft einen Mann, der sich ein Football-Spiel anschaut (widergespiegelt in den Gläsern seiner Sonnenbrille). Ungewöhnlich auch, dass die 7-UP®-Flasche bloß teilweise zu sehen war. Die ausgefallene Bildsprache gab zu denken und enthielt eine zusätzliche Botschaft. Ein mutiger Schritt. Nach und nach zeigten sich immer mehr Anzeigen von originellen Einfällen inspiriert. Es entstanden auch echte Klassiker mit raffinierten Headlines, die in das allgemeine Unterbewusstsein einsickern sollten. Viele waren harmlos, einigen fehlte sogar jeder Pep. Das trifft vor allem auf Slogans für Zigaretten zu, etwa für Lucky Strike®: „Show Me a Filter Cigarette That Really Delivers and I'll Eat My Hat!" Der schwerfällige Wortschwall wurde unvergesslich durch das dazugehörige Foto eines attraktiven Models mit angebissenem Hut. Ein anderes Motiv dieser langlebigen Werbekampagne zeigt eine Vietnamesin, die unter dem traditionellen Strohhut hervorlächelt – vielleicht eine Anspielung auf das geopolitische Engagement der Vereinigten Staaten, die den südostasiatischen Markt mit Zigaretten zu Dumping-Preisen überschwemmten.

Manche Anzeigen gelten heute als Klassiker, weil sie einen Lifestyle propagierten, der dem Zeitgeist entsprach. So machte die Clairol®-Werbung das Haarefärben zur gesellschaftlichen Pflichtübung für jede Frau und unterstrich mit dem Slogan „Does She Or Doesn't She, Only Her Hairdresser Knows", wie einfach und effektiv Färben mit Clairol® war.

Werbung wird nie neutral sein. Stets muss sie behaupten, dass eine Sache besser als eine andere ist, und auch diese andere Sache soll selbstredend die Beste sein. In den Sechzigern nahm man Abschied von aggressiven Werbestrategien. Anstatt die Verbraucher mit schalen Phrasen und Bildern zu erschlagen, versuchte man nun mit kreativer Verspieltheit ihre emotionale Einstellung zur Werbung zu verbessern. Und das funktionierte. Ganz unabhängig von den jeweiligen Methoden, mit denen die einzelnen Anzeigen auch in diesem Buch operieren: Als Rückgrat jeder kapitalistischen Marktwirtschaft verfolgt die Werbung natürlich ein ganz simples Ziel. Es gilt, einen so hohen Grad der Wiedererkennung zu erreichen, dass die Konsumenten bejubeln, ersehnen und verlangen, was immer man ihnen verkaufen möchte. Und genau das ist – auf einen kurzen Nenner gebracht – die „Big Idea".

La publicité des années 60 :

C'est quoi la Grande Idée ?

par Steven Heller

Si les publicités contenues dans ce volume étaient les uniques sources à la disposition de l'historien pour étudier et analyser les turbulentes années 60, il en émergerait une image de la culture américaine bien éloignée des réalités sociales et politiques de l'époque. Car où sont les Noirs, les Latinos et les Asiatiques ? Vues d'ici, les années 60 n'auraient pas connu les manifestations pour les droits civiques, ni la guerre du Viêtnam, le sexe, la drogue ou le rock'n roll. Ces publicités sont exhumées des cryptes de Madison Avenue, telles qu'elles ont été momifiées dans les magazines grand public de ces années-là. Elles sont aseptisées, homogénéisées, cautérisées. Cela ne signifie pas qu'elles soient dépourvues de style, de goût ou d'humour.

Mais la publicité vise à surpasser toute concurrence possible en intelligence, en savoir-faire et en volume de vente, quels que soient les moyens, pourvus qu'ils s'inscrivent dans une doctrine de prétendue « vérité publicitaire » – concept qui reviendrait à admettre la présence d'une quantité acceptable de poils de rat dans notre nourriture. De plus, les Américains d'après-guerre sont merveilleusement conditionnés à croire tout ce que racontent les médias, et toute réclame est acceptée sans la moindre remise en question.

Au cours de cette période, la publicité passe des textes longs et ampoulés aux slogans et images incisifs et pleins d'esprit, selon la méthode dite de « la Grande Idée ». Cette expression dénote à la fois un changement radical par rapport au passé, et un genre spécifiquement américain, consistant à promouvoir l'esprit de créativité. Les pionniers de la prétendue « Révolution créative », d'où émerge le concept de la Grande Idée, comprennent que pour capter l'attention du public et imposer des messages durables, il faut amuser. Donc, pour garder le public en éveil, Madison Avenue fait sonner la charge de ses meilleurs créatifs.

Un bombardement continu de slogans et d'images réduit la résistance et garantit la reconnaissance du produit vanté. Si ce dernier tient réellement ses promesses, tant mieux. Mais cela n'est pas nécessaire, surtout si la bataille est sans adversaire. En témoignent les publicités pour certaines des plus grandes marques de l'époque : Maidenform®, Anacin®, General Electric et Clairol. Tandis que les produits font efficacement leur travail, leur aura fabriquée et leur fausse mythologie confèrent à chacun, une stature et un attrait commercial tels, qu'ils peuvent s'assurer une forte part de marché, jusqu'au moment où ils en viennent à être contestés par une puissance mythologique plus formidable encore. Le sort de produits existants est souvent modifié par des campagnes publicitaires plus astucieuses, mais aussi plus acharnées, tandis que de nouvelles marques prospèrent grâce à ce que l'argot de Madison Avenue appellera du « créatif » spectaculaire.

Ainsi, dans les années 60, la Grande Idée rend la publicité plus intelligente, plus drôle et plus divertissante que jamais. De nouvelles règles sont fixées par les enfants prodiges de Madison Avenue, tels les directeurs artistiques George Lois, Gene Federico, Bill Taubin, Helmut Krone ou Bob Gage. Tous s'ingénient à capturer la force inhérente à une bonne typographie et à une imagerie forte, pour donner une certaine classe à des publicités qui, loin de mépriser les masses, leur accordent le plus grand des respects. Les années 60 sont une période de transition au cours de laquelle la Révolution créative s'attaque à la médiocrité en place. La publicité pour Dr Pepper (Poivre), boisson sans alcool, dont l'objectif déclaré est de siphonner des parts de marché à Coca-Cola® et Pepsi®, et qui montre une jeune fille assoiffée rêvant d'une deuxième bouteille de Pepper, est une affaire coûteuse pour son agence. Pourtant, une publicité pour 7 UP®, qui a autant à gagner que Dr Pepper d'un message direct et bien ficelé, utilise une approche et une expression beaucoup moins conventionnelles : au lieu d'une photographie ou d'une peinture réaliste, l'agence utilise, astucieusement, une illustration conceptuelle où un homme regarde un match de football (à travers le prisme de ses jumelles), tandis que la bouteille est à peine suggérée (alors que, par convention, dans ce genre de publicité, on montrait le produit). Cela donne au spectateur un message supplémentaire à méditer, et c'était ça l'astuce. Peu à peu, les annonces de produits de consommation sont injectées de pointes d'originalité.

Les années 60 donnent naissance à leurs propres classiques construits sur des titres et des slogans astucieux, destinés à s'infiltrer dans le subconscient des masses. Beaucoup restent inoffensifs, d'autres insipides. Parmi ces derniers, les plus mémorables sont souvent ceux consacrés aux cigarettes, comme celui-ci, pour les cigarettes à bout filtre Lucky Strike : « Montrez-moi une cigarette filtre qui mérite son titre et je suis prêt (e) à avaler mon chapeau ! » Si la blague semble laborieuse, elle devient inoubliable quand elle est accouplée à la photo d'un ravissant mannequin, coiffé d'un chapeau auquel manque un grand morceau, emporté par une morsure. Dans cette campagne, qui dure longtemps, une autre publicité montre une Viêtnamienne qui sourit timidement sous son couvre-chef traditionnel en paille, et ce sera l'un des rares petits coups de chapeau, si l'on peut dire, à l'engagement politique américain en Asie du Sud-Est (vu, entre autres, comme terrain idéal pour écouler la surproduction de cigarettes).

Certaines annonces sont considérées comme des classiques parce que, d'une manière ou d'une autre, elles ont favorisé un style de vie devenu partie intégrante de l'esprit du temps. La publicité pour Clairol, par exemple, impose à chaque femme la nécessité sociale de changer sa couleur de cheveux, et le slogan « Le fait-elle ou pas ? Il n'y a que son coiffeur qui le sait ! » souligne à quel point c'est facile et efficace.

La publicité ne sera jamais neutre. Pendant les années 60, la définition de la vente offensive passe à une créativité malicieuse, dont le but avoué consiste à mieux faire entendre la publicité. Mais indépendamment de la méthode, les publicités présentées dans cet ouvrage – véritables vecteurs de l'économie capitaliste – sont régies par une priorité élémentaire : parvenir à une identification si évidente que le public va réclamer, désirer et exiger tout ce qu'on veut lui vendre. C'est cela, en un mot, la Grande Idée.

La publicidad en los años sesenta:

¿qué es la Gran Idea?

por Steven Heller

Si un historiador utilizara como única fuente de referencia los anuncios incluidos en este volumen para examinar y analizar los turbulentos años sesenta, obtendría una imagen de la cultura norteamericana poco fiel a la realidad social y política de la época. ¿Dónde están los negros, los latinos y los asiáticos? Desde este punto de vista, en los años sesenta no existieron las manifestaciones a favor de los derechos civiles, ni la guerra del Vietnam, ni el sexo libre, las drogas y el *rock and roll*. Los anuncios aquí expuestos, recogidos tal y como aparecían en las revistas de amplia difusión de entonces, conforman una publicidad aséptica, homogeneizada y cauterizada, lo cual no implica que estuviera privada de estilo, buen gusto o humor, ni que no reflejara el espíritu de la época con cierta dosis de cinismo.

La publicidad, en aquella época, tenía por fin superar en ventas y reputación a la competencia por todos los medios tolerables según las doctrinas de la «publicidad veraz», un concepto afín a permitir la presencia de una cantidad aceptable de pelo de rata en productos alimenticios. Es más, a principios de los años sesenta, en plena posguerra, los norteamericanos estaban predispuestos a creer ciegamente en todo lo que aparecía en los medios de comunicación de masas y aceptaban los anuncios sin ningún tipo de cuestionamiento o duda, percibidos como una suerte de entretenimiento. Durante la década de los años sesenta, la publicidad abandonó su predilección por los textos extensos y ampulosos para sustituirlos por combinaciones de imágenes y eslóganes con gancho, aplicando un método conocido como la «Gran Idea». El término no sólo connota un punto de inflexión radical en relación con el pasado, sino que, además, define un género creativo genuinamente norteamericano. Los pioneros de la «Revolución Creativa» intuyeron que, para captar la atención del público y lograr calar en el imaginario popular, sus mensajes tenían que ser divertidos, lo cual llevó a las agencias de publicidad de Madison Avenue a hacerse con algunas armas propagandísticas, como la contratación de grandes talentos.

La imagen del arma sirve perfectamente como metáfora porque, al fin y al cabo, una campaña publicitaria no es distinta de una maniobra en un campo de batalla. Cuanto más eficaz sea la artillería, mejor sea la estrategia y mayor sea el contingente, más serán los cerebros y los corazones conquistados. El bombardeo incesante de eslóganes e imágenes redujo la resistencia y afianzó la identificación de las marcas comerciales. Si el producto vendido cumplía lo anunciado, tanto mejor; aunque, cuando la batalla no tenía contrincante, ni siquiera era necesario que lo hiciera. Basta, si no, con echar una ojeada a los anuncios de algunas de las marcas preponderantes de los años sesenta, entre ellas: Maidenform, Anacin®, General Electric y Clairol®. Aunque los productos eran verdaderamente eficaces, los falsos mitos que los envolvían les concedían un atractivo para las ventas que les reportaban una amplia cuota de mercado, hasta que otro fabricante los desafiaba con un producto rival aún más impresionante. El destino de los productos existentes cambiaba de rumbo cuando una nueva marca lanzaba una campaña más perspicaz e implacable, haciendo gala de lo que en el argot de Madison Avenue se conoce como «creatividad» espectacular.

A lo largo de los años sesenta, la Gran Idea dotó la publicidad de una inteligencia, humor y elegancia jamás vistos en el pasado. Los *wunderkinder* (chicos maravillosos) de Madison Avenue sentaron nuevas bases. Directores artísticos como George Lois, Gene Federico, Bill Taubin, Helmut Krone, Bob Gage y otros muchos supieron apreciar el poder inherente a la tipografía y las imágenes de calidad, y dotaron sus anuncios de un toque de elegancia que les valió el respeto del público. No obstante, sus singulares anuncios no eran sino auténticas perlas en medio de un gran magma de burdas piedras. La década de los sesenta fue un período de transición en el que la Revolución Creativa se enfrentó a un status quo mediocre.

Por ejemplo, un anuncio de refrescos Dr. Pepper® de principios de los sesenta supuso algo más que un arduo trabajo para la agencia que lo creó. Mostrando a una joven sedienta que soñaba con beberse otro Pepper, la marca intentaba arañar una parte del mercado a Coke® y Pepsi®. En cambio, el anuncio de 7 UP® recurrió a un enfoque expresivo mucho menos convencional: en lugar de utilizar una fotografía o una ilustración realista, rompió esquemas al usar una ilustración conceptual de un hombre viendo un partido de fútbol en la que la botella del refresco apenas aparecía esbozada, lo cual transmitía un mensaje que invitaba a la reflexión.

Poco a poco, los anuncios para el gran público empezaron a exhibir mayores dosis de originalidad. Pero los años sesenta también incubaron sus clásicos, con titulares elaborados y coletillas concebidas para conquistar el subconsciente del público general. Muchas de estas frases eran inocuas; otras, sencillamente insípidas. Entre las últimas, las más memorables eran los eslóganes de cigarrillos, entre ellos el de Lucky Strike®, que rezaba «Prometo que el día que encuentre un rubio de verdad, me comeré el sombrero». Pese a la rigidez aparente de la redacción, el lema calaba hondo al aparecer estampado sobre la fotografía de una atractiva modelo tocada con un sombrero mordido. En uno de los anuncios de esta extensa campaña, una vietnamita sonreía bajo un sombrero de paja típico de su región, en lo que tal vez suponía una insinuación de la implicación geopolítica de Estados Unidos en el Sudeste Asiático. Algunos anuncios se consideran clásicos porque, de algún modo, impulsaron un estilo de vida que se convirtió en parte del espíritu de la época. Los anuncios de Clairol, sin ir más lejos, lograron convertir los tintes de pelo en un imperativo social para toda mujer, gracias al eslogan «¿Se tiñe o no se tiñe? Sólo su peluquera lo sabe», que subrayaba lo fácil y eficaz que resultaba teñirse el pelo.

La publicidad nunca será neutra, ya que su fin es demostrar que un producto es mejor que otro, o aún más: que el producto anunciado es el mejor. Durante los años sesenta se redefinió el concepto de ventas agresivas: se pasó de bombardear al consumidor con imágenes populares a recurrir a juegos creativos destinados a que el público se sintiera más incentivado. Y funcionó. Pero, independientemente del método que emplean, los anuncios ilustrados en este volumen respondían a una única meta: construir una imagen comercial incomparable y perfectamente identificable por el público que suscitara el clamor, el deseo y la demanda, al margen de cuál fuera el producto vendido. Y, en pocas palabras, ésa es la Gran Idea.

1960年代の広告：

ビッグ・アイデア？　だから何だっていうんだい？

スティーヴン・ヘラー

もし、この本に掲載された広告が、後世の歴史家が激動の1960年代を検証し、分析する際に残された唯一の遺物だとしたら、そこから浮かび上がってくるアメリカの姿は、当時の社会的、政治的現実とは似ても似つかぬものになっただろう。黒人は、ヒスパニックは、アジア系の人々はどこへ行ってしまったのか？　広告という見晴台から眺める限りにおいては、60年代には公民権運動も、ベトナム戦争も、セックスやドラッグ、ロックンロールさえも存在していなかったことになる。少なくとも、何か有意義な形では。マディソン街における広告業界の地下室にしつらえられた霊廟から掘り起こされ、大衆雑誌によってミイラ化されたこれらの広告は、好ましくない部分は削除され、均質化され、麻痺させられたものなのだ。そうかといって、決して趣味が悪いわけでもユーモアのセンスに欠けているわけでもない。

この時代の広告は、何がなんでも競合相手をうち負かそう、よりたくさん売ろうという目的のために立案され、いわゆる「広告的真実」という教義の許容範囲内でさえあれば、いかなる方法論も存在し得るものである。それは、食べ物に混入したアンダーヘアがどの程度の量までなら許せるか、といった議論にも似たコンセプトであったりする。さらに、第二次世界大戦後のアメリカ人は、60年代前半当時、マスメディアが送り出すものなら何でも喜んで信じることに慣れ親しまされていたから、疑問やためらいを持つこともなく広告を受け入れていた。

60年代、広告は、「ビッグ・アイデア」と呼ばれる方法論のもと、黎明期の冗長で大げさなものから、簡潔でウィットに富んだキャッチコピーと映像の組み合わせへと進化していった。この言葉は、過去からの急激な変化と、きわめてアメリカ的なプロモーション形式というふたつの意味を内包している。いわゆる創造革命の先駆者たちは、真に視聴者の心をつかみ、息の長いメッセージを伝えるためには、送り手が常に受け手を楽しませなければいけないことに気づいたのだ。そこで、大衆をずっと踊らせつづけるために、マディソン街は秘密兵器を呼び寄せなければならなかった。

スローガンとイメージの絶え間ない砲撃が、抵抗勢力を弱体化し、人々の認知を得やすくする。もしその商品が、宣伝文句に見合う内容を実際に伴っていればなおさら良いというだけの話だ。しかし、それすらも、戦う相手がいなければ必要のないことである。60年代のトップブランド——メイデンフォーム、アナシン、ゼネラル・エレクトリック、クレイロール——の広告を見てみるといい。むろん、製品そのものも悪くなかったとはいえ、まやかしの神話が彼らに威信と魅力を与え、市場で絶対的なシェアを誇っていた。より強大な存在が彼らに挑戦状を突きつけるまでであるが……。既成の製品の運命は、より洗練された、かつ容赦のない広告キャンペーンによってたびたび変更させられ、広告業界用語でいうところの華々しい「クリエイティブ」たちのおかげで、また新たなブランドが富を手にすることになるのだ。

「ビッグ・アイデア」によって、60年代の広告は明らかにそれ以前の時代に比べてずっと巧妙で、面白く、楽しい存在へと変身を遂げた。マディソン街の鬼才と呼ばれたアート・ディレクターたち——ジョージ・ロイス、ジーン・フェデリコ、ビル・トービン、ヘルムート・クローネ、ボブ・ゲイジほか——は新しいスタンダードを作り上げた。彼らは優れたタイポグラフィに内在する力をとらえ、力強いイメージとともに広告に品格をもたらし、軽蔑の代わ

りに敬意をもって大衆に接したのだ。ただ、そういった珠玉のかたわらには、常に安っぽい石ころも並んでいた。60年代は、創造革命が旧態然とした凡庸さと闘っていた過渡期でもあった。60年代初頭に繰り広げられたソフトドリンクの広告のなかで、コークとペプシのシェアを少しでも吸い取ろうとしたドクターペッパーが送り出した広告は、のどの乾いた若い女がペッパーを夢に見るというものだったが、広告代理店にしてみれば出費のかさんだ試みだったはずだ。

　しかしながら、セブンナップは、もう少し型破りな表現方法を採用した。写真や写実主義的な絵に代わって、ある男がフットボールの試合（彼が手にした双眼鏡のレンズに映っている）を見ているというコンセプチュアルなイラストが使用されたが、そこにはドリンクボトルの影すらなく（こういった広告の場合、商品を見せるのがしきたりだった）、見る側に考える余地を残したのだ。これは勇気のある行為だったと言えよう。ゆっくりと、マスマーケット向けの広告にも独創性が持ち込まれようとしていた。

　60年代には、大衆の潜在意識に働きかけて口車に乗せようという奸智にたけた見出しとキャッチフレーズの古典的作品が誕生している。その多くは無害で面白みのないものだった。それでも、タバコのスローガンのなかにはいくつか記憶に残る作品がある。たとえばラッキー・ストライク・フィルターの「うまいフィルター付きタバコがあったら、帽子を食べてやる！」だ。言葉づかいそのものは格好いいとは言えないが、ムシャムシャと食べたあとのある帽子を頭にのっけた魅力的なモデルの写真と結びついたときに、忘れがたい印象を残す。

　長く続いたこのキャンペーン中、あるときは伝統的な麦わら帽子の下でおどおどと微笑むベトナム人女性が登場したが、アメリカの東南アジアに対する地政学的な干渉（大量の吸い殻のゴミ捨て場にしたことも含めて）に言及した数少ない例だったろう。

　ある種の広告は、時代精神の重要な一部を構成するライフスタイルを促進したという意味で古典となった。たとえばクレイロールの広告は、すべての女性にとって髪の色を変えることが社会的にも不可避であるかのような風潮をもたらし、「彼女はしている？それとも？秘密を知っているのは美容師だけ」というスローガンが、髪を染めることがいかに簡単で効果的かを強調した。

　広告は決して中立にはなりえない。常に、ある特定のものがもう一方よりも優れているということ、なおかつその特定のものが最高のものであることを立証しなければならないからだ。60年代、「売り込み」の定義は、陳腐な言葉とビジュアルを駆使して頭ごなしに消費者をやりこめようというものから、受け手が広告を好きになれるようにという意図のもと、創造的でちゃめっ気のあるものへと変化した。そして、その手法はうまくいったのだ。しかし、いずれにしても、本書中の広告は──間違いなく市場主導型の資本主義経済の中軸をなすものだ──たったひとつの単純な計画表によってつき動かされている。すなわち、大衆とは売られているものなら何であれ騒ぎたて、欲望し、要求する存在であるという比類なき認識を築き上げること。つまり、それこそが「ビッグ・アイデア」だったのだ。

this calls for

Budweiser®

the
neighbors... out in the kitchen,
swapping ideas with good friends. This is fun
...and this calls for Budweiser.

Where there's life...there's Bud.
KING OF BEERS · ANHEUSER-BUSCH, INC. · ST. LOUIS · NEWARK · LOS ANGELES · TAMPA

Smirnoff, 1967 ◄ *Budweiser, 1962*   ► *Schlitz, 1960*

Invitation from your Tavern Keeper:
COME AND WATCH THE RACES!*

"We've got a winner!"

Schlitz and your tavern keeper invite you to see the season's three big races at your neighborhood tavern. Bring along your friends to join the fun. Wherever people of good taste get together you're sure to find Schlitz. It's brewed like no other beer in the world—brewed with just the kiss of the hops for superb flavor.

THE BEER THAT MADE MILWAUKEE FAMOUS

move up to

* Schlitz presents all three on CBS-TV!

Kentucky Derby, May

Preakness, May 21

Belmont Stakes, June

Shakespeare's Works,
the Mini-dress and Gordon's Gin.

Ah, the great things England
has given us all.
Think that over, as you
sip a martini made with
glorious Gordon's dry gin.
Created by Alexander Gordon
in England, 1769.

Gordon's Gin

Biggest selling gin in England, America, the world.

PRODUCT OF U.S.A. 100% NEUTRAL SPIRITS DISTILLED FROM GRAIN. 90 PROOF. GORDON'S DRY GIN CO. LTD., LINDEN, N.J.

What will the English think of next?

Lucky Strike Filters will show you plenty.
Plenty of flavor. Plenty of fine tobacco.
L.S./M.F.T. Lucky Strike means fine tobacco.
And now, Lucky Strike means filter tip.

Product of The American Tobacco Company

"Show me a filter cigarette that really delivers taste and I'll eat my hat!"

Lucky Strike, 1966

▶ *White Owl, 1965*

If I were a man, I'd smoke White Owl Miniatures.

If you *are* a man,
take up with the small, trim, good-looking
cigar that makes you look good.
White Owl Miniature . . .
the little one.

Chesterfield

KING

Cigarettes

LIGGETT & MYERS TOBACCO CO.

There is a cigarette for the two of you. L&M.

©1969 Liggett & Myers Incorporated

Chesterfield, 1961 ◄ *L&M, 1969*

"Us Tareyton smokers would rather fight than switch!"

Join the Unswitchables. Get the filter that made Activated Charcoal famous—and the taste that makes Tareyton smokers so aggressively loyal.

Fine
granules of
<u>Activated Charcoal</u>
in pure
cellulose

The white filter gives you clean taste

The charcoal filter gives you smooth taste

Together they give you the great taste of
DUAL FILTER TAREYTON
America's largest-selling Activated Charcoal filter cigarette
Product of *The American Tobacco Company — Tobacco is our middle name* ⊙ A. T. Co.

**NOW
IN NEW
POP-OPEN
PACK**

Tareyton, 1964

And the winner is...

Where in the World Have You Been?

The space program was a great vehicle for advertising numerous products, but in this particular instance some creative art director clearly missed the point. Let's see. How can we sell more vodka? How about dressing a model in a space suit, pile her hair in a mass of loopy curls, and throw in some antennas. Space and booze. Yeah, that should send consumers flocking to the liquor store.

Wo um alles in der Welt warst du denn?

Die Raumfahrt war ein genialer Aufhänger für Produktwerbung aller Art. Aber hier ist der Artdirector wohl übers Ziel hinausgeschossen. Nach der Devise „Wie verkaufen wir mehr Wodka?" hat er ein Model in einen Raumanzug gesteckt, ihre Dauerwelle turmhoch auftoupiert und ein paar Antennen durchgesteckt. All und Alk, wunderbar – da werden die Käufer natürlich sofort in die Schnapsläden stürmen.

Mais sur quelle planète vivez-vous donc ?

On sait que la publicité a mis le programme spatial à toutes les sauces, mais dans l'exemple qui nous occupe, un créatif a manifestement raté son but. Voyons – comment vendre davantage de vodka ? Et bien on habille un mannequin d'une tenue spatiale, on amasse ses cheveux en volutes bouclées où l'on pique des antennes pour faire réaliste. Et le tour est joué. Voilà qui va envoyer des légions de consommateurs dans les magasins de spiritueux.

¿En qué mundo vives?

El programa espacial constituyó un vehículo sensacional para anunciar numerosos productos, si bien, en este caso, algún director de arte de dudosa creatividad dejó claro que no había entendido nada. Veamos su planteamiento. ¿Cómo podríamos vender más vodka? ¿Qué tal si vestimos a una modelo de astronauta, le recogemos el pelo a modo de casco y le ponemos un par de antenas? Sin duda, plantear una odisea de alcohol para alentar a los consumidores fue una idea poco brillante...

いったいどこの世界に行ってたの？

宇宙計画は、数々の商品の宣伝手段としても大いなる役割を果たしたが、この広告の場合、"クリエイティブ" なアートディレクターの焦点は明らかにずれてしまったようだ。そうだなあ。もっとたくさんウォッカを売るにはどうしたらいい？　モデルに宇宙服を着せて、素頓狂なカールの山を頭にのせて、アンテナを2本ってのはどうかな。宇宙と酒。いいねえ。これで消費者が酒屋に押しかけること間違いなしだ。

HAVEN'T TRIED SMIRNOFF? WHERE IN THE WORLD HAVE YOU BEEN?

You've really been out of touch if you haven't explored Smirnoff with orange juice, with tomato juice, with 7-Up® (in the new Smirnoff Mule). Or discovered that Smirnoff makes the dryest Martinis, the smoothest drink on-the-rocks. Only Smirnoff, filtered through 14,000 pounds of activated charcoal, makes so many drinks so well. Why wait? Let the next Smirnoff launching be *yours!*

Get acquainted offer: Try the delicious drinks you've been missing with this new half quart sampler bottle. Now available in most states.

Always ask for *Smirnoff* It leaves you breathless®
VODKA

Smirnoff, 1966

Cadillac

THE CADILLAC "V" AND CREST interpreted in Rubies and Diamonds BY HARRY WINSTON.

Where Craftsmanship is a Creed!

There are, to be sure, many ways to learn the story of Cadillac craftsmanship. But the best of these—and certainly the most enjoyable —is simply to inspect and drive a 1960 Cadillac. Every exquisite detail of its interior, for instance, reveals a skill and care in execution that is unique in motordom. Every graceful, tight-fitting body line evidences the rare devotion lavished on its final assembly. And every silent, solid mile on the highway speaks eloquently of Cadillac's great overall soundness of construction. We suggest you visit your dealer soon—and see for yourself how fine a motor car can be when craftsmanship is the irrevocable creed of its maker.

18th Century embroidery from The Brooklyn Museum   The Fleetwood 60 Special   Jeweled "V" and Crest created by Cartier

*The highest praise that can be accorded any product in any field
is to declare it the Cadillac of its kind.*

CADILLAC MOTOR CAR DIVISION, GENERAL MOTORS CORPORATION

Cadillac, 1960

Are they making the turnpikes shorter this year?

Take that next trip in a '61 Plymouth. This Solid Beauty will give you a feeling that roads have never been so smooth, horizons so easy to catch. Everything about this low-price car takes you there in new comfort. It's easy to get in, easy to sit in, easy to see out of. Its quiet one-piece welded Unibody is snug and tight. Its Torsion-Aire suspension (no extra cost) takes practically all the sway and dip out of driving. Plymouth is smoothing the kinks out of the m... Let your Plymouth dealer show you h...

61 PLYMOUTH...SOLID BEAUTY

A CHRYSLER-ENGINEERED PRODUCT. *Enjoy "The Garry Moore Plymouth Show" and "The Garland Touch" each week on CBS Television.*

What makes a Pontiac so eager to go?

This Catalina has more horsepower per pound than any other automatic transmission car made in America. (As much as one horse per 10.65 pounds.) That's an ideal balance between weight and power. Gives you hustle when you need it. Improves gas mileage, too. Eager to go? Go see your fine Pontiac dealer.

PONTIAC MOTOR DIVISION · GENERAL MOTORS CORPORATION

THE ONLY WIDE-TRACK CAR Pontiac has the widest track of any car. Body width trimmed to reduce side overhang. More weight balanced between the wheels for sure-footed driving stability.

Plymouth, 1961 ◄   *Pontiac, 1961*

Meet the *Scout*!

A whole new idea in low-cost transportation...

Here's America's new quick-change artist. In minutes you can make your INTERNATIONAL Scout whatever kind of vehicle you want. The cab top, doors and windows are readily removable; the windshield folds down. No other vehicle is so changeable *and* so storm-snug. Then there's the full-length Travel-Top. Now the Scout can become a multi-purpose delivery unit or convertible, a light-duty pickup or runabout.

It's a working partner, a pleasure companion. You can buy the new Scout with two-wheel-drive or four-wheel-drive,

depending on the roads you travel or the jobs you want done. Take your friends hunting in rough country, take the family on a picnic, haul loads. And the Scout is compact: less than 13 feet overall, 100-inch wheelbase, 68 inches wide, 67 inches high. New INTERNATIONAL Comanche 4-cyl. 90 hp. engine goes easy on gas, oil, and upkeep.

Let your imagination roam—isn't the Scout the only one that spans *all* your needs? Your INTERNATIONAL Scout Dealer or Branch is the place to go to find out everything you can do with the Scout.

This is the Scout, a neat, nimble pickup with 5-ft. long loadspace.

Same Scout with cab top off. Takes you only minutes to remove.

Same Scout stripped, with doors and windows off, windshield down.

Same Scout for delivery work with optional full-length Travel-Top.

International Harvester Company, Chicago

Strike a blow for originality!
(Take the Mustang Pledge.)

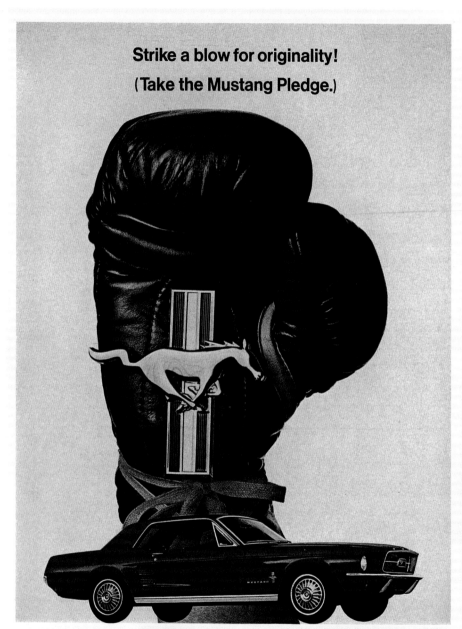

Still the original and lowest-priced car of its kind with bucket seats. **MUSTANG** *Ford*

Ford, 1967

*The XP-755 Chevrolet Corvette Shark: 102.1" wheelbase, 152.2" overall, 327-cubic-inch displacement, V-8 engine featuring Roots-type supercharger, 4 side-draft carburetors developing over 400 horsepower.

Shark by Chevrolet–ACtion sparked by AC

The same AC Spark Plugs that add power to this car of tomorrow are available for your car today! Engineers specify ACs for experimental cars like the Corvette Shark because of AC's self-cleaning Hot Tip. It heats faster to burn away fouling carbon deposits — delivers longer peak power — greater economy for *every* car! Don't experiment with your spark plugs, ask for ACtion . . . ask for AC.

AC SPARK PLUG ⊕ THE ELECTRONICS DIVISION OF GENERAL MOTORS

**FIRE-RING
SPARK PLUGS**

AC Spark Plugs, 1963

The new Mercedes-Benz 220 SE Coupe photographed at Helbrun Castle in Austria

Coupe d'Etat

For over half a century, it has been the pleasure of men of state to drive or be driven in a Mercedes-Benz. Mercedes-Benz now offers its newest car, a veritable coupe of state, to the discriminating few who can afford to be seen in this, the finest of machines. It is the new 220 SE coupe with a fuel injection engine, optional power steering and a choice of automatic or four-speed transmission. Its interior is completely hand-fitted with elegant leather and wood embellishments and represents the best of the coachmaker's art. There is no similar car in the world. It combines sports-like performance with the dignity of diplomacy. Further, it carries its silver three-pointed star in the restful silence of complete discretion. That, of course, is entirely in keeping with the seventy-five-year-old tradition of Mercedes-Benz.

Mercedes-Benz Sales, Inc., South Bend, Indiana *(A Subsidiary of Studebaker-Packard Corporation)*

Thunderbird, 1962 ◄　*Mercedes-Benz, 1962*　　　　　　　　　　　► *Concrete, 1960*

over 160 mph...under $5000

Avanti: The Maximum Car. Over 160 mph...under $5,000. No other car—at any price—carries Avanti's record-making supercharged V8...obeys Avanti's racing-type disc brakes...struts Avanti's head-turning aerodynamic shape. Avanti: America's only high-performance 4-passenger luxury car. Apply at your Studebaker dealer's.

From the advanced thinking of  **Studebaker** CORPORATION

Avanti, 1963

The Coupe de Ville · Jeweled "V" and Crest created by Cartier

Cadillac splendor

Even the most brilliant occasions seldom surpass in splendor
the Cadillac journey that takes you there.

Cadillac Motor Car Division · General Motors Corporation

Cadillac, 1962

▶ Pontiac, 1963

Ugh.

This is an awful picture of a Volkswagen. It's just not us.

We don't go in much for trading bees or sales jamborees or assorted powwows.

Maybe it's because we don't quite understand the system.

We've never figured out why they run clearance sales on brand new cars.

If there are cars left over every year, why make so many in the first place?

And how come the price goes down, even though the cars are still brand new?

How does the poor guy who bought one last week feel about this week's prices?

Imagine what a problem it must be to keep enough parts on hand when they're always changing. And for the mechanic to keep track of what he's doing.

It's all very confusing.

Either we're way behind the times. Or way ahead.

meet a history maker...

ALL NEW

ALL 'JEEP'

'JEEP' WAGONEER

Different? Definitely!

The new 'Jeep' Wagoneer is the first station wagon ever built to offer the comfort, silence, speed and smoothness of a passenger car—plus the safety and traction of 4-wheel drive.

The Wagoneer is the one family wagon you can drive almost anywhere, in almost any kind of weather.

It's the first and only 4-wheel drive wagon with optional automatic transmission and independent front suspension.

The 'Jeep' Wagoneer features the power and economy of America's first and only automotive overhead camshaft engine, the Tornado-OHC.

It has the most usable cargo space...both high and wide. It's also available in 2-wheel drive models. Step in. Size it up. Try it out at your 'Jeep' Dealer's today!

Exploring inner space

Small spaceman makes big discoveries about Ford interiors

Scene: Ford showroom. While his parents choose their '63 Ford, the astronaut explores. ■ First surprise — Swing-Away steering wheel moves over, make

Bright idea — illuminated glove compartment. Spaceman likes bucket seats (will recommend them for school bus). ■ Door lights! Red warns traffic, whi

For major space problems: Ford wagons — most loadspace in low-price field. ■ High-flying compact: Falcon Sprint with tachometer, sporty steering whee

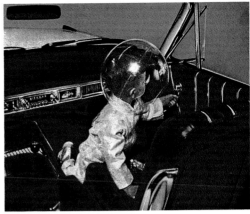

ntry easy (for adults, too). ■ Spaceman inspects console, plush carpeting, sporty floor-mounted shift, crank-vent windows — finds all systems GO (in luxury).

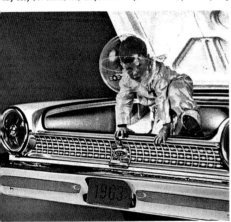

ghts your way in. ■ Space booster: roomy, well lined, illuminated trunk. ■ Fairlane is rated A-O.K. (Note to spaceman's mother: Ford vinyl is soil-resistant).

■ The beautiful exteriors of today's Fords are matched by beautiful interiors. And this beauty isn't just a thin veneer of glamor — it's solid, substantial luxury. ■ Example: Ford's deep-pile carpeting outlasts ordinary car carpeting because it has extra nylon and more loops per square yard. ■ Ford vinyl is heavier, more durable than the vinyl used in other cars. ■ Ford interiors are protected against weather and noise by one-third more insulation than America's other best-selling car. ■ And Fords are designed for comfort. Door openings are higher and wider than other cars in Ford's field . . . passenger space is more than in some medium-price cars. ■ Before you decide on any new car, explore a 1963 Ford — inside and out.

America's liveliest, most care-free cars

FORD

FALCON · FAIRLANE · FORD

Spaceman's final report to nation: all Ford interiors are . . . out of this world.

FOR 60 YEARS THE SYMBOL OF DEPENDABLE PRODUCTS · *Ford* · MOTOR COMPANY

Rambler takes off – the Marlin comes on.
Meet America's first man-size sports-fastback!

You're looking at the most exciting Rambler ever built—Marlin! A car unlike anything else on the scene today. Here's too much automobile to be just another fastback—too much luxury to be just another sport car—too much solid value to be anything but a Rambler. You get dazzling performance, including the might of a 327 cu.-in. V-8 option. You get Power Disc Brakes and individually adjustable reclining front seats, *standard*. You get a choice of practically any sports option you can name, like floor shifts, console, bucket seats, wire-wheel covers—plus *all* the solid extra-value features Rambler provides at no extra cost, such as Deep-Dip rustproofing, Double-Safety Brakes (separate systems, front and rear)—and more. Catch the Marlin in all its excitement—at your Rambler dealer *now*. In limited production, but stepping up fast. American Motors—Dedicated to Excellence

Marlin By Rambler

Phillips 66, 1965

Psssst. Tell your wife it's a family car.

MARLIN '66: Even with buckets* it seats six in comfort. Sizzling fastback power... two 6's, three V-8's
Coil-spring seats and Double-Safety brakes (like Cadillac). See it quick at your friendly Giant-Killer
your American Motors / Rambler Dealer. American Motors... where quality is built in, not added on

*optional

The Wizard of Aah's...
new 1966 Fairlane convertible!

1966 Fairlane GT Convertible

Now Fairlane swings out with a great new look, an eager new personality, a wide new range of models— including three of the newest convertibles on the road! You get the idea when you take your first look at the '66 Fairlane GT convertible. Standard equipment includes bucket seats, sporty console, specially sporty GT identification and wheel covers, big 390 cubic-inch V-8,

and more. GT has options like GT/A, which means Sportshift Cruise-O-Matic, our new automatic transmission that you can also shift like a manual. Some car! New this year too are an XL convertible, a Squire wagon with Magic Doorgate (swings open like a door for people *and* swings down like a tailgate for cargo!). This year we re-invented Fairlane. Drive one today and see!

AMERICA'S
TOTAL PERFORMANCE CARS

FORD

MUSTANG·FALCON·FAIRLANE·FORD·THUNDERBIRD

Body By Fisher, 1966 ◄◄   Rambler, 1966 ◄   Ford, 1966

Scrambler 160

Trail 90

Rally

The Honda Custom Group. You take your pick of customized Hondas at your dealer's. The models feature a special type of tank, pipe, handlebars, seat. You get your bike the way you want it. A real blast. What'll Honda think of next? Keep tuned in. The Rally (above) is part of the new Custom Group.

See the "Invisible Circle" color film at your local Honda dealer's. While you're there, pick up a color brochure and safety pamphlet, or write: American Honda Motor Co., Inc., Dept. QQ, Box 50, Gardena, California 90247. © 1967, AHM.

Honda, 1967

Honda shapes the world of wheels

Honda has more fresh ideas than boys around a bikini. High-jacket pipes, rally tanks, racing seats. Custom color jobs that are positively psychedelic. Excitement runs right through the line. Even the classic models show it. That famous four-stroke engine comes on with authority. Won five out of five '66 Grand Prix Championships. An all-time record. A bike for a boss. That's Honda. Anything less would question your manhood. One of those 20 models is going to turn you on. Brace yourself.

HONDA

You meet the nicest people on a Honda.

And the winner is...

Here's the Ideal Transportation for Two People *plus*

Blame it on bad styling or bad timing. Whatever the reason, the ungainly sight of a miniature car in the midst of overblown Detroit monsters was an instant thumbs down by the American public. Ahead of its time perhaps? Within a few years another sub-compact from Germany would eclipse America's love affair with massive cars and usher in the era of the convenient and economical compact car.

Das ideale Transportmittel für zwei ...

Schlechtes Timing? Schlechtes Styling? Wie auch immer. Inmitten der Dickschiffe aus Detroit war das unschöne Miniaturauto beim amerikanischen Publikum ein glatter Flop. Vielleicht war es seiner Zeit ja zu weit voraus. Nur ein paar Jahre später stahl allerdings ein deutscher Kleinstwagen den großen amerikanischen Schlitten die Schau und leitete die Ära praktischer, preiswerter Kleinwagen ein.

Voici le moyen de transport idéal pour deux personnes plus

Peut-être s'agit-il d'une erreur de style, ou alors le moment était mal choisi. Allez savoir. En tout cas, le public américain a instantanément refusé de voir cette drôle d'automobile miniature au milieu des monstres boursouflés de Detroit. Etait-elle en avance sur son temps? En l'espace de quelques années une autre petite voiture, allemande celle-là, fera oublier aux Américains leur amour pour les grosses cylindrées et marquera l'entrée dans l'ère de la petite voiture pratique et économique.

El transporte ideal para dos personas

¿Una estética inadecuada en el momento equivocado? Por el motivo que fuera, la visión de un biplaza entre los gigantescos vehículos de Detroit provocó el rechazo del público norteamericano. Quizá este modelo se adelantó a su tiempo... Al cabo de pocos años, otro vehículo compacto procedente de Alemania eclipsaría el romance de los estadounidenses con los coches de grandes dimensiones y daría el pistoletazo de salida a los automóviles utilitarios, más asequibles y fáciles de manejar.

2人プラスαのための理想的な移動手段がここに

悪いのはスタイリング、それともタイミングか。理由はともあれ、大げさな作りのデトロイト製巨大アメ車の群れの中にたたずむ小型車というぶざまな光景は、すぐさまアメリカ人によって却下された。時代の先を行き過ぎたのだろうか？ それから数年のうちに、ドイツからやってきた別のサブコンパクトカーが、アメリカ人と大型車とのラブ・アフェアに影をおとし、便利で経済的な小型車時代の到来を告げることになる。

Join the "Personal Car" Set

IMPORTED

Metropolitan "1500"

World's Smartest Smaller Car

Here's ideal transportation for two people *plus*—with almost 50-inch front seat hip room. And the rear occasional seat is handy for smaller children, pets or packages. Comes in smart convertible and hardtop models.

Conceived and engineered in the U.S. to provide comfort you're used to, the Metropolitan "1500" is built in England to European standards of craftsmanship. The peppy 55 H.P. engine provides thrilling responsiveness with top economy—*perfect* for around-town driving or turnpike cruising.

Join the Personal Car Set soon. You'll enjoy owning and driving a car so appropriate for your *personal* motoring needs. Parts and service available coast to coast.

TEST-DRIVE THE "MET" AT YOUR RAMBLER-METROPOLITAN DEALER

FILE PROT ON | LOAD REWIND | UNLOAD | TAPE IND ON

SELECT   RESET   START   READY

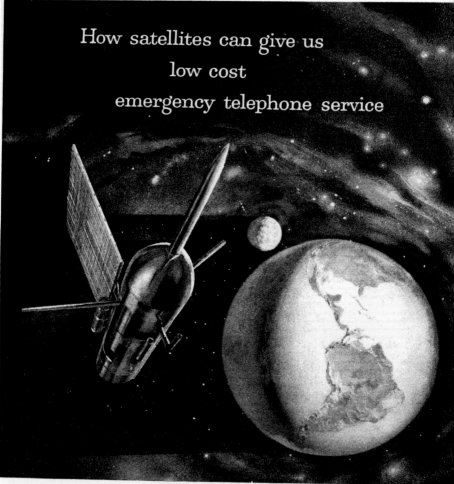

How satellites can give us low cost emergency telephone service

Beyond their immediate military necessity, our present rocket and missile programs promise many vital peacetime benefits to us all...

Well past the drawing board stage are plans to use satellites as a low-cost emergency stand-by system to relay telephone calls around the world.

Your call would be beamed to a satellite, then bounced back to a receiving station on Earth. Cost is estimated at a fraction of what must be spent to install and maintain cables or radio relay towers.

While satellite telephone service is still in the future, *Thor*—the rocket that can put it into being—is thoroughly proved. Built by Douglas, maker of the DC-8 jetliners, *Thor* has been successful in more than 90% of its shots. It is key booster in the "Discoverer" firings and launched the first nose cone recovered at ICBM range.

Thor is another product of the imagination and experience gained by Douglas in 20 years of missile development.

Launched by the Douglas-built *Thor* IRBM, satellites like this would relay telephone messages anywhere in the world without costly cables or towers.

DOUGLAS

MISSILE AND SPACE SYSTEMS
MILITARY AIRCRAFT • DC-8 JETLINER
TRANSPORT AIRCRAFT • AIRCOMB
GROUND SUPPORT EQUIPMENT

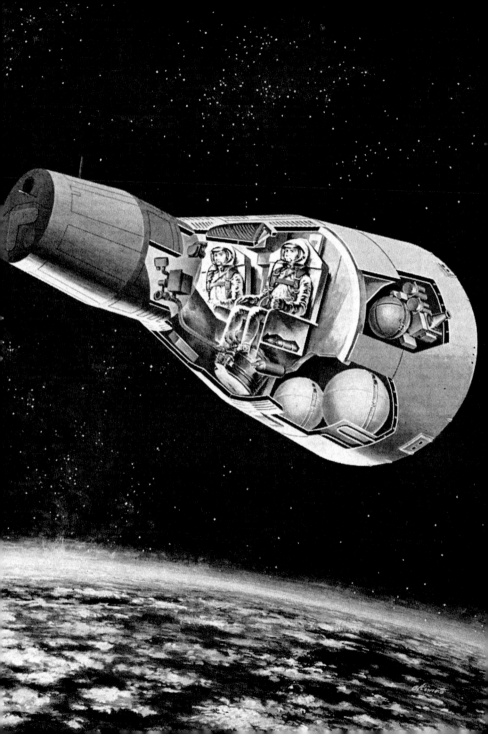

this is the new IBM Electric

IBM

It's new—inside and out, with 28 engineering achievements that bring you typing at its finest! Your secretary will love its alive, eager response. You'll admire its styling and high-volume output. For this— is the most handsome, efficient typewriter made.

IBM, 1960

► Monroe, 196.

It's the Compact . . . compact in appearance and in fact. And notice . . . the compactness is between the keyboard and the carriage. All the dead air space has been engineered out. But the important work areas are set up the same as in other electrics. The carriage is a full 12 inches and the return is electric—automatic. The keyboard, too, is full size (and with new features). This is the whole idea—compactness. This is American engineered compactness—a more efficient product to do the job and so a more efficient price —$225*. Available in three decorator colors and all the crisp type styles you'll ever need. See the Compact today. Call your local Smith-Corona Marchant representative, or mail coupon on opposite page. *Plus tax

the compact office electric by Smith-Corona Marchant: $225*

S C M SMITH-CORONA MARCHANT

Smith-Corona, 1961

angry young computer

Our B 200 can outdo any computer in its class. Any computer, regardless of name or initials. So naturally, when it sees a system being bought or leased on the <u>basis</u> of name or initials, the B 200 gets angry. Because it knows it can do a better job for fewer dollars. If you know anybody who's considering a computer, do him a favor. Mention the Burroughs B 200. The same goes for anybody who's angry at his present computer. And we hear a lot of people are. Burroughs—TM

Burroughs Corporation

See a Burroughs computer in action, Election Night, ABC·TV.

Photo courtesy United Air Lines

Why do major airlines serve soft drinks in cans? For the very same reason you'll switch some day soon.... convenience. Cans take less space.... easier to store. Cans weigh less.... easier to carry. They chill faster. Rugged, too. And no deposits, no returns! Convinced? Pick up a dozen of your favorite soft drinks.... in convenient cans.

BETHLEHEM STEEL

U.S. Steel, 1961 ◄   *Bethlehem Steel, 1963*

The indestructible Nauga.

Sadder but wiser mothers pray for permanent furniture. The Nauga answers those prayers. With the hide off his back. Naugahyde vinyl fabric. Naugahyde is so tough, it breaks a kid's spirit. So comfortable, it gets overused. So durable, the kids are old before it is.

With Naugahyde you can sail past the Jones's. It can look like the most expensive ▲ fabrics. Linen. Tweed. Silk. Leather. Wood.

Brocade. Burlap! Bamboo! 500 bewildering varieties and every single one is Naugahyde.

Look for the imaginary Nauga and find beautifully indestructible furniture. His picture is hanging on every piece of real Naugahyde. If you ➤ can't find the Nauga, find another store.

The Nauga is ugly, but his vinyl hide is beautiful.

*Naugahyde is Uniroyal's registered trademark for its vinyl upholstery fabric.

Naugahyde
vinyl fabric

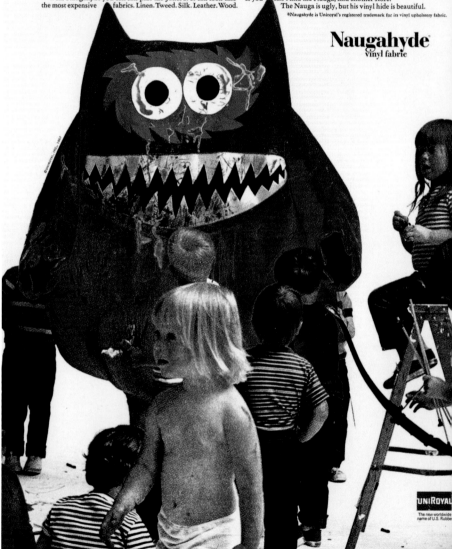

Bigelow, 1964 ◄ *Naugahyde, 1967*

HOLY BATMASK!

To get this all-new, all-color Batmask FREE, all you have to do is take your father or mother or aunt or uncle or grandmother or grandfather down to your participating G-E TV dealer.

Hey! He'll even show you how it flips over and turns you into Robin.

GENERAL ⚡ ELECTRIC

Just in time for Halloween—Only from General Electric **TV** dealers.

General Electric, 1966

Architects: Robert A. Hoesler, William C. Muchow / General Contractor: A.A. & E. B. Jones Co.
Engineers: Ken R. White, Inc. / Owners: J. W. Anderson & Co.

DENVER ADOPTS NEW IDEA FOR CONTROLLING INDOOR CLIMATE...

Inland Radiant Comfort System is an integral part of Denver's new Lincoln Tower Building now being erected. This highly advanced concept separates ventilating from heating and cooling — and eliminates the need for moving large amounts of air by forced circulation. ■ Uniform, draft-free heating and cooling (acoustical control, as well) are provided by radiant ceiling panels. Ventilating air is carried through raceways in the cellular steel floor, as are electrical wiring circuits. Air is chemically treated — and humidity brought to the optimum comfort point. ■ Other advantages of the Inland Radiant Comfort System — such as savings of rentable floor space and ductwork — are too numerous to mention here. More information is available in the booklet, "Breakthrough in Office Comfort Control". Write for it today.

member of the INLAND steel family **Inland Steel Products Company** *Engineered Products Division*
4109 WEST BURNHAM STREET, MILWAUKEE 1, WISCONSIN   EP-37A

Inland Steel Products Co., 1964

▶ *Avisco Cellophanes, 1964*

We're still building airplanes around people.

McDonnell Douglas DC-8s and DC-9s, chosen by more than 60 of the world's leading airlines, were designed to please the passenger. Now, our Douglas Aircraft Company is creating new dimensions in jet travel with the jetliner of the Seventies: the DC-10. The DC-10 will offer unsurpassed levels of comfort and convenience. It continues a tradition of commercial aircraft design, performance, and dependability which has progressed — without interruption — since 1933.

MCDONNELL DOUGLAS

McDonnell Douglas, 1969

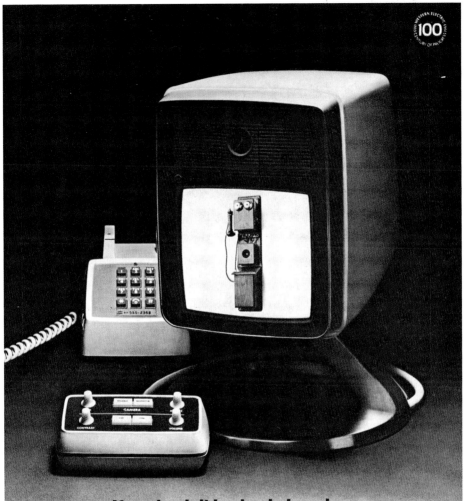

If we hadn't looked ahead...
...we wouldn't have anything to look back on.

Carrier pigeons and smoke signals were good ways to get the word around when Western Electric went into business just 100 years ago. And a loud shout was still the best carrier for the spoken word.

But before long, Mr. Bell's invention changed the world. Soon we were building telephones. Today, equipment made by Western Electric has helped make the Bell network the most advanced communication system in the world.

And inventions by engineers for Bell Labs and

Western Electric are still changing things. The Picturephone® set above, is a phone of tomorrow being developed today. And we can't even picture what the phone will be like over the next 100 years.

We make Bell telephones.

But we've also made our share of communications history.

Western Electric
MANUFACTURING & SUPPLY UNIT OF THE BELL SYSTEM

And the winner is...

Now Producing Electricity from the Power of the Atom
Through a concentrated public relations blitz, atomic optimism reached its crest by the 1960s. The benefits of nuclear power were being heralded as the salvation for a power-hungry American public. And of course it was "a peacetime dream come true." What wasn't advertised was the potential for terrorist threats and a bleak nuclear future realized by disasters such as Three Mile Island and Chernobyl.

Neuer Strom vom Atom
Nach intensiven Public-Relations-Kampagnen erreichte die nukleare Euphorie in den sechziger Jahren ihren Gipfel. Die Kernenergie wurde als Rettung für das energiehungrige amerikanische Volk bejubelt. „Ein Friedenstraum wird wahr", hieß es. Was fehlte, war ein Wort zu den Risiken durch Terrorismus und dräuende Atom-GAUs à la Harrisburg und Tschernobyl.

Maintenant le pouvoir de l'atome peut produire de l'électricité
Porté par un faisceau concentré de relations publiques, l'« optimisme atomique » atteignit son apogée au cours des années 60. Les aspects bénéfiques du nucléaire étaient annoncés comme le salut qu'attendait un public américain affamé de pouvoir. Et évidemment c'est « un rêve de paix qui vient vraiment ». Pas de publicité pour le potentiel qu'il représente aux mains des terroristes et pour l'avenir sombre qu'illustreront les catastrophes de Three Mile Island et de Tchernobyl.

Producimos electricidad con energía atómica
Gracias al bombardeo de publicidad, el optimismo atómico alcanzó su punto álgido en los años sesenta. Las ventajas de la energía nuclear se anunciaban como la salvación a la sed de energía del público estadounidense. Aquélla fue «una era de paz en la que los sueños se hicieron realidad». Sin embargo, lo que no se anunció fue que la energía nuclear podía suscitar amenazas terroristas y deparar un futuro sombrío, provocando desastres como el de Chernóbil.

原子力で電気を作り出しています
集中的な一大広報キャンペーンの甲斐あって、原子力に対する楽観主義は、1960年代にそのピークに達した。原子力がもたらす恩恵は、エネルギーを渇望するアメリカ国民にとっての救世主として歓迎されたのだ。確かにそれは「平時の夢の実現」だったかもしれない。しかし、宣伝文句に書かれていなかったのは、テロの脅威と、スリーマイル島やチェルノブイリの惨事で現実のものとなった、原子力エネルギーを待ち受ける暗い未来だった。

Picture shows the Yankee Atomic Electric
Plant at Rowe, Mass. operated by a group of
New England investor-owned companies.

ATOMIC ELECTRIC POWER IS HERE
A PEACETIME DREAM COME TRUE...

On this quiet New England river you see just one of the American plants that are now producing electricity from the power of the atom.

Operated by the investor-owned electric light and power companies, they form a striking demonstration of America's use of "Atoms for Peace."

Not so long ago it was just science fiction—getting electricity from the power of the atom.

Today atomic power is actually cooking suppers . . . running TV sets . . . heating, lighting and cooling for many home and business customers of the investor-owned electric light and power companies.

These companies are already operating 5 atomic electric plants. They are spread across the country from New England to California. More are being built.

All over the country, the investor-owned companies carry on research and development on new ways to produce electricity. It is part of their nationwide program to make certain America always has a plentiful supply of power. They can supply all the additional electricity the future will call for.

Investor-Owned Electric Light and Power Companies | *Keep America Powerful*

Company names on request through this magazine

Investor-Owned Electric Light and Power Co., 1961

✿✿✿ *All-American Ads 6os* **Consumer Products** ✿✿✿ *All-American*

FRESH FROM MOTOROLA..

Cheetah, 1968 ◄ Motorola, 1962

new leader in the lively art of electronics

Old-fashioned reliability comes back in style in modern Motorola® TV

For that spot in your living room where you now have an old TV set that has a genius for conking out during your favorite program, there's a new Motorola that will not only fit in nicely, but also keep giving you a clear, sharp picture until that last ornery cattle rustler gets what's coming to him, and you're ready to call it a night.

Take the TV-Stereo Hi-Fi combination at the left. Your wife will be partial to the beautiful Drexel cabinet (a Motorola exclusive), but you're more likely to appreciate the exclusive

Golden Tube Sentry Unit, protecting the tubes against destructive warm-up power surges, main cause of tube failure. That's one reason why Motorola—and only Motorola—guarantees* all tubes and parts on every model for a full year, instead of the usual 90 days.

You can have this famous Motorola reliability in the type and size TV you want (with or without remote control) in a TV-Stereo combination, console, table model or portable. Prices start as low as $139.88**

◀ This country living room, created by Eyvind Earle, achieves an exciting linear pattern through the imaginative use of glass walls, louvered doors, and wooden beams. Motorola's TV-Stereo Hi-Fi combination is taken from Drexel's *Declaration* grouping.

New Motorola Console from Drexel's ▶ *Touraine* collection features sliding tambour doors, 23-inch screen (overall diag. meas.; 283 sq. in. viewing area), and Golden Satellite® Remote Control.

MOTOROLA

Manufactured in Canada by Seabreeze Manufacturing Ltd., licensee

New Motorola Console with fine-furniture styling.

New Motorola Table TV with 23,000 volts of picture power.

hold the future in your hand
with **SONY**
RESEARCH MAKES THE DIFFERENCE

THIS IS TELEVISION OF THE FUTURE. This is the personal set predicted for the decade of the Seventies. So light and compact you carry it with you like a book, wherever you go. Put it beside your bed, on your desk at the office, outdoors for picnicking on the patio, in the back of the car or on the boat. It plays anywhere on its own rechargeable battery pack, auto battery or AC, with a picture so bright and sharp ordinary sets pale by comparison. Weighing only 8 lbs., it is hardly larger than a telephone, yet it out-

performs standard receivers in sensitivity and durability. Available only in limited quantities, SONY brings it to you today through its advanced research in the epitaxial transistor, so powerful and sensitive it is used only in computers and other advanced electronic equipment —and the new Micro-TV. It would be no exaggeration to say that someday all TV will look like SONY Micro-TV. But why wait for someday? See it today at selected dealers. SONY Micro-TV list $229.95. Optional battery pack.

See and hear the world famous SONY all-transistor, battery operated radios at selected dealers.
SONY CORPORATION OF AMERICA 514 Broadway, New York 12, N.Y.
In Canada: General Distributors Ltd. 791 Notre Dame Ave., Winnipeg.

Now, enjoy all the excitement of color in the brightest, most true-to-life RCA Victor Color TV ever...from $399⁹⁵*

Lifelike natural color. New Vista® Color TV for 1965 gives you the most true-to-life RCA Victor Color ever . . . with better color purity, greater contrast than ever before. Color is so bright, so lifelike, you have to see it to believe it! Crisp, clear black and white pictures, too. Automatic Scene Control for balanced brightness and contrast.

Most widely proved—dependable. RCA pioneered and developed Color TV—made it a reality—proved it in homes like yours across the country. It's the most widely proved Color TV you can buy. Today, it's America's first choice—more people own RCA Victor than any other TV—black and white or color.

*New low price. Now only $399.95 for the *Darcy*, not shown. Manufacturer's nationally advertised price, optional with dealer. All prices, specifications subject to change.

 RCA The Most Trusted Name in Television

RCA Victor, 1964

► *Sony Television, 1967* ►► *Motorola, 1962*

Our new stereo won't add any distortion to their sound.
And it won't take any away, either.

When you listen to hard rock, it's not the easiest thing in the world to tell where the sitar ends and the distortion begins. But we at Sony have a new stereo that can help slightly. It's the HP-580.

With it you get FM/AM and FM stereo in the tuner section, 8-inch woofers, 3-inch midranges, and 2-inch tweeters in the speaker section, and a Pickering cartridge in the cartridge section.

It has a Dual 1210 turntable, extremely sensitive FM stereo

separation, a high filter switch, loudness control, and specially designed Sony transistors that fit our specially designed electronic circuits. (Niceties you don't usually get from a stereo short of going out and buying components.)

So the Cream won't sound sour. The Strawberry Alarm Clock won't sound piercing.

And because of its built-in dust cover and dustamatic brush, the Rolling Stones will gather no moss.

Nothing-but-the-truth Stereo.
The Sony® HP580

©1969 Sony Corp. of America. Visit our showroom, 585 Fifth Avenue, New York, N.Y. 10022.

FOLK ROCK IS A DRAG

hagström guitars

Hagstrom Guitars

SALVADORE DALI : This enlargement was made from an actual 60-second Polaroid Land picture. Notice the exceptional quality in detail and tone— characteristic of pictures taken with Polaroid's new panchromatic films. Inci-

dentally, the newest of these films has the amazing speed of 3000. It lets you take superb 60-second pictures indoors without flashbulbs. Polaroid Land Cameras are priced from $76.85. See your dealer for a demonstration.

Polaroid, 1960

What's a beautiful girl like you doing with a heavy duty detergent like this?

the whole wash, of course! With new Cold Power, there's nothing to it!
In cold water, new Cold Power coaxes the meanest dirt out of anything London, Paris or
Seventh Avenue can dream up, whether it's a synthetic or natural fabric.
With Cold Power and cold water, there's none of the shrinking, fading, color running or
stain setting you get with hot water. And Cold Power doesn't just take care of your
fashions. It also does the job for everything else you wash. Everything...even slipcovers.
New Cold Power! greatest invention since fashion went washable.

© 1967 Colgate-Palmolive Co.

Cold Power Detergent, 1967

Homeroom.

This is the place.
A place you can decorate all by yourself
With crispy no-iron sheets that match
fringed bedspreads and fluffy towels.
Cannon Royal Family makes stuff like t
And Cannon would like a place in your plac
So why don't you look us up
the next time you're in town.

CANNON
ROYAL FAMILY

Cannon® Sunflower towels, bedspreads and sheets (50% cotton, 50% polyester) in pink, blue, orange or green. At fine department stores. Cannon Mills, Inc., New York 10020

Cannon, 1969

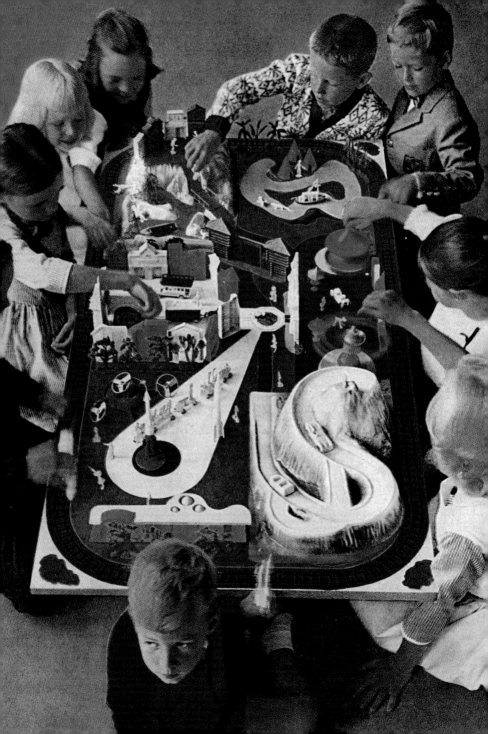

MAKE IT ALL COME TRUE!

Burgerbits Dog Food, 1962 ◄ *Kal Kan Dog Food, 1963*

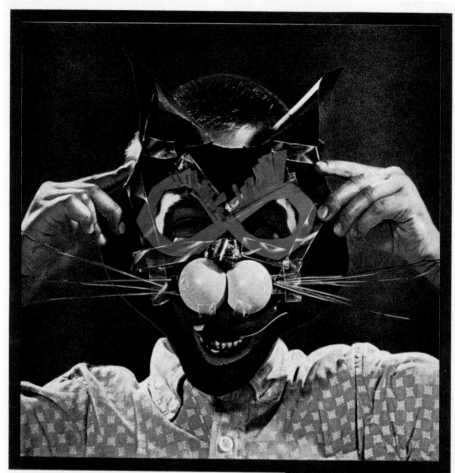

How your kids can have a happier Halloween

Boo! The trick is to treat them to transparent "Scotch" Brand Tape . . . to make a mask, a witch's hat, a magic wand—even create the entire costume with crepe paper and tape. Or to play *tape*-the-tail-on-the-cat (no dangerous pins!). Grownups can help: tape penny candy in wax paper for treating callers —tape paper pumpkins, fall leaves, scary things to windows and mirrors for a true Halloween look. The other 364 days, too, "Scotch" Brand Tape is sharp as a witch's wand at making fun come true. Keep it handy all year 'round for the kids—and for *you!*

3M MINNESOTA MINING & MANUFACTURING CO.
. . . WHERE RESEARCH IS THE KEY TO TOMORROW

© 1961 3M Co., St. Paul 6, Minn.

*When tape costs
so little, why
settle for less
than the best—
"Scotch" Brand
in the plaid
dispenser*

Next time, buy two—one for the kids and one for you!

These **STAR SAPPHIRE** cherished jewels **RUBY** have inspired **BLACK PEARL**

the world's most beautiful bowling balls

Jewels Courtesy of C. D. Peacock – Jewelers in Chicago for 125 years

✴the CROWN✴JEWEL✴
with Miracle Tracking Action!

The shimmering, star-like beauty of the Crown Jewel is matched only by its startling performance. The first truly new bowling ball in 50 years, it is made of a gem-like new material that grips the lane with unprecedented sureness. Bowl a Crown Jewel and see how firmly it holds the course you set for it regardless of lane conditions. We call it Miracle Tracking Action. To bowl your best this season, have your franchised Brunswick dealer fit you for a new Crown Jewel Bowling Ball now. You have a choice of sapphire blue, ruby red or black pearl, $39.95.

The No. 1 Name in Bowling
Brunswick

Jewels by Trifari, 1960 ◄ *Brunswick, 1962*

Some people even *United* can't help!

If you can pack your possessions on the back of a bike, you won't have much use for our services. Not that we have anything against people traveling light. It's just that United's "Pre-Planned" moving service was meant for families who have everything . . . including the big problem of getting it all safely to a new home.

We've added special wrinkles like Sanitized* vans to keep a family's possessions fresh and clean. We've

taught our packers to treat each fragile item like an heirloom when they place it in our custom built containers. And we've made "new city" information free and easy to get through our Bette Malone Moving Consultant Service. So even though we can't be of immediate service, we hope you'll keep us in mind. We're easy to find in the Yellow Pages under "MOVERS."

Serving the United States, Canada and 114 Foreign Lands

UNITED MOVES THE PEOPLE WHO MOVE THE WORLD!

*Reg. U.S. Pat. Off.

United Van Lines, 1969

▶ *OMC Boats, 1963*   ▶▶ *Schick Hairdryer, 1963*

NEW FROM OUTBOARD MARINE...

THE BEST THING THAT'S HAPPENED TO WATER IN YEARS!

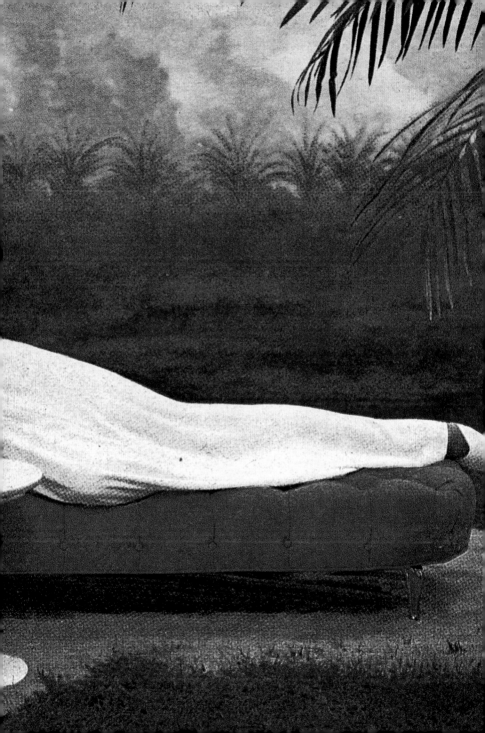

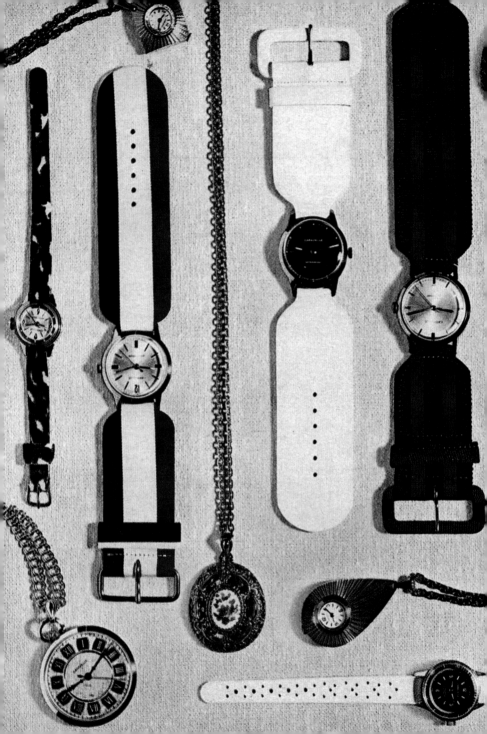

Western Electric is crossing a telephone with a TV set.

Someday you'll be a star!

What you'll use is called, simply enough, a Picturephone® set. Someday it will let you see who you are talking to, and let them see you.

The Picturephone set is just one of the communications of the future Western Electric is working on with Bell Telephone Laboratories.

Western Electric builds regular phones and equipment for your Bell telephone company. But we also build for the future.

Western Electric
MANUFACTURING & SUPPLY UNIT OF THE BELL SYSTEM

General Electric, 1969

Capitol Records, 1968

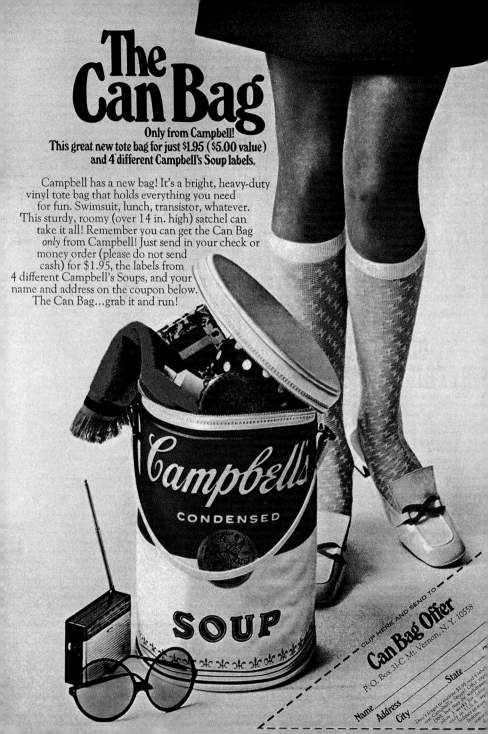

And the winner is...

... And a Tribe of Colors
Two for the price of one. This ad for blankets managed to subjugate woman as well as stereotype Native Americans in a silly portrayal that had fashion models posing as squaws in need of comfort by way of a modern electric blanket.

Eine tolle Kriegsbemalung ist das ...
Zwei zum Preis von einer. Diese Werbung für Heizdecken schlug gleich doppelt zu, sie setzte Frauen herab und zementierte das Klischee vom Indianer. Das alberne Bild zeigt Mannequins als komfortversessene Squaws, die sich für elektrische Decken erwärmen.

,.. Et des couleurs pour toute la tribu
Deux pour le prix d'une. Cette publicité pour des couvertures cible aussi bien les femmes que les Amérindiens standards dans un portrait stupide qui montre des mannequins posant comme des squaws avides de confort – rien de tel qu'une couverture électrique moderne.

... Una tribu de colores
Dos por el precio de uno. Este anuncio de mantas logró subyugar tanto a las mujeres como al estereotipo de los amerindios nativos, ofreciendo uno de los retratos más absurdos de la publicidad. Las modelos, tocadas de indias, posaban envueltas en una moderna manta eléctrica que les aportaba la comodidad de la que carecían.

多種多色そろえて…
一つ分のお値段でもう一つ差し上げます。この毛布の広告は、ファッションモデルたちを、現代的な電気毛布に安らぎを求める "インディアン娘" に仕立て上げるという馬鹿馬鹿しい手法によって、女性と、ステレオタイプなネイティブ・アメリカンという二者を同時に隷属させることに成功してしまった。

Turn on Indian Summer
to brave a chilly night

with *Sunbeam* electric blankets

Gentle, feather-light warmth to chase
the chills away; lighted, graduated heat
control; machine-washable. All sizes, and
a tribe of colors: Tropic Pink, Harvest Gold,
Avocado Green and Surf Blue.

Custom Deluxe in 100% acrylic comfort,
infinite heat settings, 5-year guarantee.*

Deluxe blankets in a blend of 65% polyester,
35% rayon; 9 heat settings, 2-year guarantee.*

Sunbeam

built with integrity—
backed by service

Beautifully
packaged for
gift giving.

Sunbeam, 1969

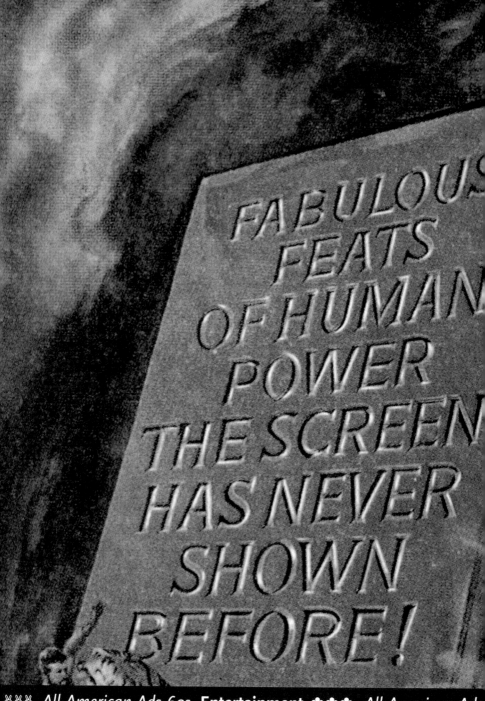

FABULOUS
FEATS
OF HUMAN
POWER
THE SCREEN
HAS NEVER
SHOWN
BEFORE!

SP[
OF

Hercules Unchained, 1960 ◄ The Impossible Years, 1968

NOTHING YOU HAVE EVER WITNESSED BEFORE HAS PREPARED YOU FOR SUCH SHEER STABBING SHOCK!

ALFRED HITCHCOCK'S "The Birds"

TECHNICOLOR

"It could be the most terrifying motion picture I have ever made!" —ALFRED HITCHCOCK

starring
ROD TAYLOR · JESSICA TANDY
SUZANNE PLESHETTE

and introducing
'TIPPI' HEDREN
a fascinating new personality

Screenplay by EVAN HUNTER · Directed by ALFRED HITCHCOCK · A Universal Release

Based on Daphne Du Maurier's classic suspense story!

SOON AT MOTION PICTURE THEATRES ACROSS THE NATION!

he Birds, 1963

▶ *Barbarella, 1968*

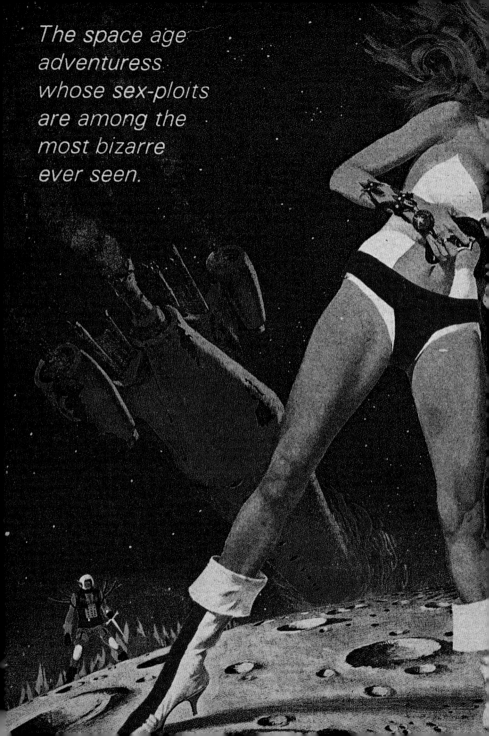

The space age
adventuress
whose sex-ploits
are among the
most bizarre
ever seen.

PARAMOUNT PICTURES presents
A BHE FILM
The
FRANCO ZEFFIRELLI
Production of
ROMEO
& JULIET

No ordinary love stor

Romeo & Juliet, 1968

Mutiny On The Bounty, 1962

ELVIS PRESLEY & NANCY SINATRA

smooth,
fast
and in
high
gear!

Torrid
together...
singing...
dancing...
turning on
the romance...
as they make
the speed-scene
at the famed
furious
Charlotte 600!"

HEAR
ELVIS
SING

his greatest
new songs on the
RCA VICTOR
soundtrack album

METRO·GOLDWYN·MAYER
Presents
"SPEEDWAY"

see it soon
at a theatre
near you!

Also Starring
BILL BIXBY · GALE GORDON · CARL BALLANTINE
Written by   Directed by   Produced by
PHILLIP SHUKEN · NORMAN TAUROG · DOUGLAS LAURENCE
PANAVISION AND METROCOLOR MGM

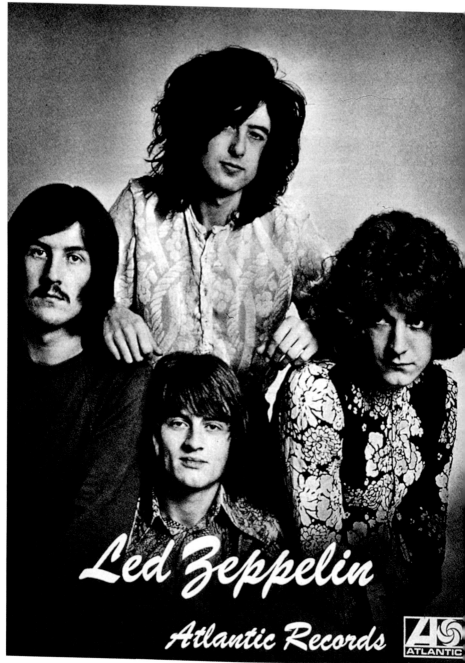

Led Zeppelin

Atlantic Records

Country Joe & The Fish, 1968

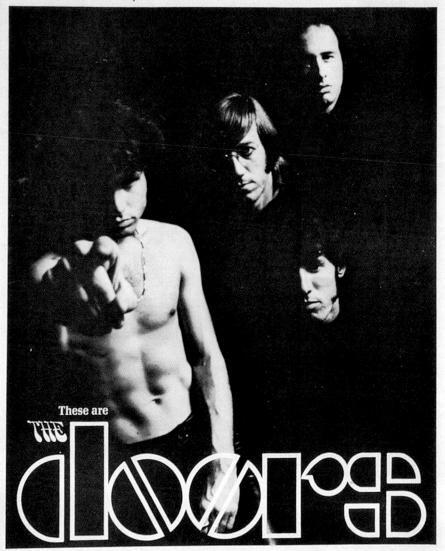

These are
THE doors

Their second super-album, STRANGE DAYS, is now available. Look for it carefully—because THE DOORS are not exactly on the cover. But they sure as hell are inside.

elektra   ELEKTRA RECORDS, 1855 BROADWAY, NEW YORK, N.Y. 10023

ne Doors, 1967

And the winner is...

We, the Japanese, are in a Better Position
Telling it like it is from first hand experience, this Japanese import film predicted what damage a nuclear holocaust would cause "as realistically as possible". Produced so that it would "serve the cause of peace", it was no doubt released in response to the paranoia surrounding the Cuban missile crisis. You can be sure this is one movie whose weekend receipts weren't among the top ten.

Die Japaner müssen es ja wissen ...
Welche Verwüstungen ein nuklearer Weltenbrand anrichtet, das bekam man „so realistisch wie möglich" in diesem Filmimport aus Japan vor Augen geführt. Produziert „im Dienste des Friedens", war er in Zeiten der Kuba-Krise wohl als Antwort auf die um sich greifende Paranoia zu verstehen. Sicherlich kein Kassenschlager.

Nous, les Japonais, sommes bien placés pour le dire
Jouant sur l'expérience de première main du peuple nippon, ce film japonais d'importation prédit « de manière aussi réaliste que possible » quels dommages causerait un holocauste nucléaire. Produit pour « servir la cause de la paix », il fut sans aucun doute lancé pour répondre à la paranoïa entourant la crise des missiles à Cuba. Vous pouvez être sûr que les gens ne se sont pas bousculés pour le voir le week-end.

Nosotros, los japoneses, lo sabemos mejor que nadie
Hablando sin tapujos a partir de experiencias de primera mano, esta película de importación japonesa predecía de la manera «más realista posible» el daño que un holocausto nuclear podría causar. Producida con objeto de «servir a la paz», la película se lanzó en respuesta a la paranoia que suscitó la crisis de los misiles cubanos, aunque, como es de suponer, no se formaron largas colas para verla.

我々、日本人には誰よりもその資格があります
日本から輸入されたこの映画は、核による大量殺戮がいかなるダメージを与えるかということを、直接的な経験に基づいた率直な語り口で「可能な限り写実的に」予言した。「平和のために貢献すべく」製作された映画のアメリカでの公開が決まったのは、間違いなくキューバミサイル危機がもたらしたパラノイアのせいだろう。少なくとも、この映画だけは週末の興行成績トップテンに入らなかっただろうことは想像に難くない。

THE LAST WAR

A most spectacular film depicting the horrors of a nuclear war that may befall us at any moment.

"THE LAST WAR"

A statement by M. Shimizu,
President, Toho Co., Ltd. Tokyo

The time has come for us to make this picture . . .

Newspapers, radio commentators, scholars, common men — all speak of a dread hovering ominously over the entire world every second of every day. If — we repeat — if this dread should descend upon us, it will result in the destruction of mankind and, perhaps, life itself.

Men of intelligence are taking great pains to avert it. This is indeed commendable; there can never be too much effort exercised toward this end. But still we live in fear that a great war, the Last War may come.

We the Japanese are in a better position than people of any other nation to make a film such as this. We side with no one; we are inimical to no one. "The Last War" is presented as our appeal to the world.

We of the Toho Company are employing every vestige of our technical skill to represent as realistically and appealingly as possible exactly what will happen if this colossal horror befalls us.

It is our sincere hope that by producing and exhibiting this film we can serve the cause of peace.

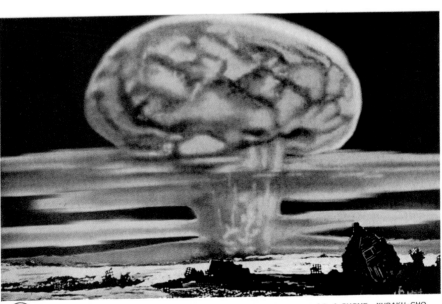

 TOHO COMPANY, LIMITED   14, 1-CHOME, YURAKU-CHO CHIYODA-KU, TOKYO, JAPAN

The Last War, 1961

Do the skate:

Skate right, clap hands.

Skate left.

Shake shoulders, roll hands.

Skaters position, lean forward.

Skate forward right, then left.

Cut loose in Career Club™ Shirts

Career Club tapered shirts in cotton broadcloth with new hi-boy roll collar. 15 hot and sweet colors. $4. Slightly higher in the West. Get free dance booklet at your Career Club dealer. Or write to Dance, Truval Shirt Co. Inc., 350 Fifth Ave., N.Y.

Dan River, 1962 ◄   *Career Club Shirts, 1967*   ► *Groshire/Austin Leeds, 1968*

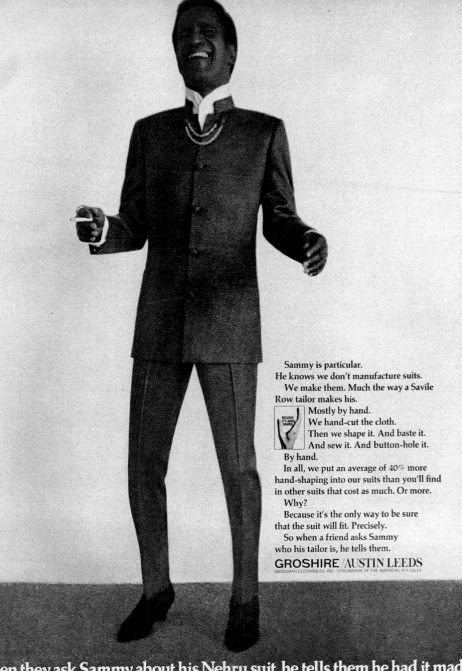

Sammy is particular.
He knows we don't manufacture suits.
We make them. Much the way a Savile Row tailor makes his.
Mostly by hand.
We hand-cut the cloth.
Then we shape it. And baste it. And sew it. And button-hole it.
By hand.
In all, we put an average of 40% more hand-shaping into our suits than you'll find in other suits that cost as much. Or more.
Why?
Because it's the only way to be sure that the suit will fit. Precisely.
So when a friend asks Sammy who his tailor is, he tells them.

GROSHIRE/AUSTIN LEEDS
GROSSMAN CLOTHING CO. INC. 1290 AVENUE OF THE AMERICAS, N.Y. 10019

hen they ask Sammy about his Nehru suit, he tells them he had it made.
And he's not putting them on.

Cut up, cut out, cut loose with Max Factor's
CALIFORNIA PINK-A-PADES

**Two pink escapades for lips and fingertips.
Two sheer...two shimmering...too tempting!**

It's the great new color adventure for summer.
Say it Pink-A-Pale (soft, feminine, fragile)
or Pink-A-Fling (lively, zingy, daring).
Wear it either super-sheer or super-frosted.
Any way you play it, have a wild
pink Pink-A-Pade!

California Pink-A-Pades by Max Factor

Max Factor, 1967

▶ *Kanekalon, 1969* ▶▶ *Fresh Start, 1966*

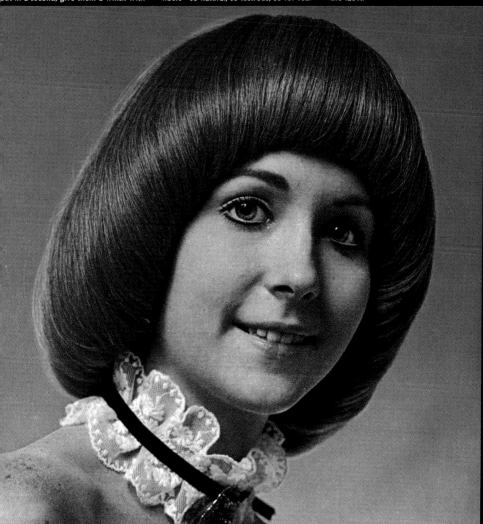

I dreamed I drove them wild in my *maidenform* bra

COUNTERPOINT*...new Maidenform bra made with super-strong Spandex — new, non-rubber elastic that weighs almost nothing at all yet lasts (and <u>controls</u> you) far longer than ordinary elastic. Exclusive "butterfly insert" adjusts size and fit of each cup as it uplifts and separates! Cotton or Spandex back. White. From 2.00.

*REG. U. S. PAT. OFF., ©1961 BY MAIDENFORM, INC.—MAKER OF BRAS, GIRDLES AND SWIMSUITS   All Cotton Broadcloth, Acetate, Cotton, Vyrene (Spandex) Elastic.

Maidenform, 1961

▶ *Coppertone, 1967*

THE
MADNESS
OF
COTTON

as expressed by Adele Simpson

Great, colorful flowers that explode like fireworks
in a white, white firmament. Cotton made it happen. Cotton
made it the high fashion it is. Wear it and
listen for the murmurs of admiration, the sighs of envy.
*National Cotton Council, Box 12285,
Memphis, Tenn. 38112.*

COMFORTABLE · CAREFREE
COTTON

THE CATALINA® MAN *discovers* Creslan®
ACRYLIC FIBER

For the golfer who takes his sports and sportshirts seriously, this handsome lightweight shirt is knit to fit in 70% Creslan acrylic fiber, 30% nylon. It lets a man swing with comfort. It dries into perfect shape after laundering. In sporting colors, about $12.95. Cyanamid makes the Creslan acrylic fiber; Catalina makes the garments. American Cyanamid Company, New York.

Color co-ordinated hosiery available from Esquire Socks.

CYANAMID

Cotton, 1967 ◄   *Creslan, 1960*

And the winner is...

Reward: You Wearing it

Never was the American bust so blatantly displayed to the public than through Maidenform's "I dreamed I was..." campaign. Confident and firmly trussed, the gals in this last of the bullet shaped brassier ads would fall victim a few years later to bra burnings and a more natural look putting to end the voyeuristic fantasies of generations of men and boys.

Belohnung: Selber tragen

Nie wurde der amerikanische Busen so penetrant ins öffentliche Blickfeld gerückt wie in Maidenforms „I dreamed I was"-Kampagne. Selbstbewusst warben straff bewehrte Mädels für die scharfen Büstenhalter. Nur wenige Jahre später wurden BHs öffentlich verbrannt und es setzte sich ein natürlicherer Look durch: Schluss mit den voyeuristischen Fantasien ganzer Generationen von Männern und Halbwüchsigen.

Récompense : vous le portez

Jamais le buste américain n'aura été exposé avec un tel aplomb que dans la campagne « J'ai rêvé que j'étais... » de Maidenform. Sûres d'elles et dûment soutenues, les minettes de la dernière publicité pour soutiens-gorge en obus seront victime des années plus tard de la vindicte des féministes et du retour à une allure plus naturelle, qui sonneront le glas des fantasmes voyeuristes de générations d'hommes de tout âge.

El premio te lo llevas puesto

Nunca el busto de las americanas se había exhibido al gran público de manera tan descarada como en la campaña «He soñado que era...» de Maidenform. Seguras de sí mismas y apuntando bien, las chicas embutidas en estos sostenes con forma de bala cayeron víctimas, años más tarde, de la quema de sujetadores y la defensa de un aspecto más natural, lo cual puso fin a las fantasías de generaciones de hombres y adolescentes.

懸賞金：これを身につけた君

メイデンフォームの「もし、○○だったらと夢想した…」キャンペーンほど、アメリカ人のバストを露骨に陳列してみせた表現もないだろう。弾丸型ブラ広告の末期を飾った、きっちりと締め上げられて自信に満ちたキャンペーン・ギャルたちは、数年後にはブラ焼きフェミニストやナチュラル・ルックのあおりを食う運命にあった。そして、多くの青少年、あるいは成人男性の覗き魔的ファンタジーも終わりを告げたのだった。

I dreamed I was

HAT BY JOHN FREDERICS

WANTED

in my Maidenform* bra

'FRAME-UP'*new bra with 3-way support

Embroidered panels frame, outline and separate the cups. Extra-firm supports at the sides give you extra uplift. Stretch band at the bottom keeps the bra snug and securely in place. It's a 'Frame-up'—in A, B, C cups.

IT'S A STEAL, AT
$1⁵⁹

*REG. U. S. PAT. OFF. ©1963 BY MAIDENFORM, INC., MAKERS OF BRAS, GIRDLES, SWIMSUITS

Maidenform, 1963

NEW FROM ALBERS!!! THE NEW LIGHT MIX
FOR REAL CREAMERY BUTTERMILK PANCAKES

Beautiful new package—wonderful new mix! Like no other. Blends rich wheat,
corn and lightest rice flours with real creamery buttermilk for special tenderness.
Discover Albers Deluxe Flapjack Mix, the new quality product from Carnation.

VISIT CARNATION EXHIBIT AT CENTURY 21 EXPOSITION • SEATTLE WORLD'S FAIR/APRIL 21 TO OCTOBER 21, 1962

Life Savers, 1961 ◄ *Albers Flapjacks, 1962*

► *Diet Imperial, 1967*

1/2
THE
CALORIES
OF REGULAR
MARGARINE

Diet Imperial is a brand-new soft spread that lets you cut calories without cutting flavor. Because you get the very same flavor ingredients of famous Imperial Margarine plus liquid corn oil, yet only $\frac{1}{2}$ the calories! Tastes so good, you'd buy it for the flavor alone. Use it on everything from asparagus to zucchini. It's a great new way to help stay yum and slim! Try new Diet Imperial soon.

Diet Imperial's taste never goes to your waist

New Diet Imperial is soft in texture so it's super spreadable! Comes in two handy new servers.

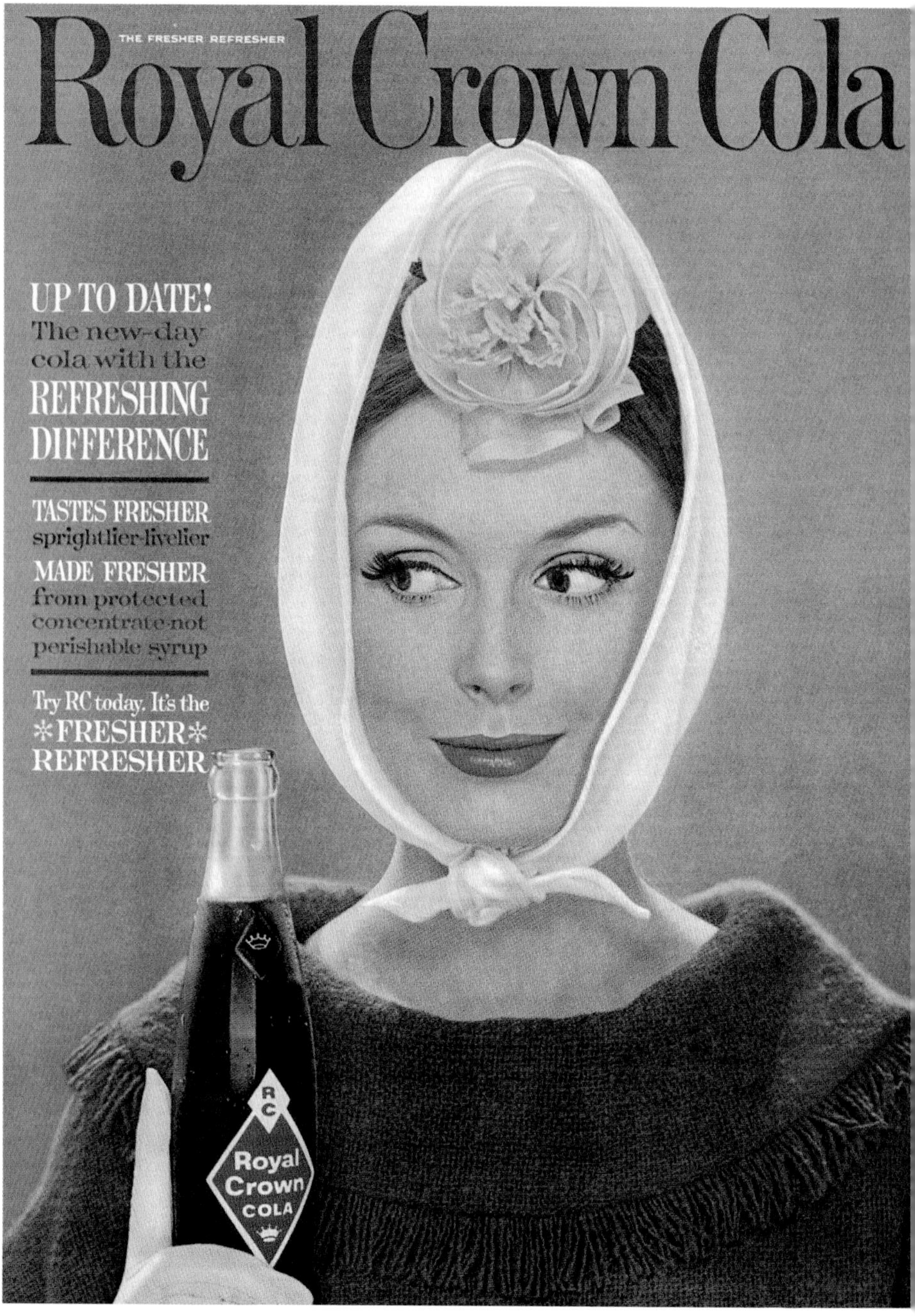

Royal Crown Cola, 1961

The Now Taste
of Tab.

Tab. Trimmed down in sweetness, so it's a little bit dry.
With 1 crazy calorie in every 6 ounces.
Like everything now a little bit crazy, but wow.
The now taste of Tab.
That's what's happening. To the nicest shapes around.

Tab Cola, 1966

LABORATORY TESTS PROVE

NOTHING IS IMPOSSIBLE
for people who drink Dr Pepper!

It is said that people who drink Dr Pepper can do <u>anything</u>: dance till dawn, have dimples when they smile, make bushels of money.

And we have a laboratory full of wealthy, dimpled dancers to prove it!

Obviously, Dr Pepper is no dull, run-of-the-mill soft drink. It tastes brighter. And it's really much <u>more</u> than refreshing; it's the real pepper-upper active folks need to keep up with the busy lives they lead.

Now that Dr Pepper is available almost every-where, there's no reason for <u>anyone</u> to fail at anything! Have a frosty bottle of Dr Pepper and face the world with a conquering heart.

* * *

Ha-Ha? We try to make Dr Pepper ads funny (more or less) so you'll enjoy reading them. But we're se-rious about wanting you to try a carton or two. Dr Pepper <u>is</u> as good as we say it is. But <u>please</u> don't take our word for it. Buy some, instead, today.

Dr. Pepper, 1960

▶ 7-Up, 196.

What's
got
into
Tang?

NEW NEW NEW

INSTANT

Tang

BREAKFAST
DRINK

More Vitamins C and A

Tang, 1961

▶ Hills Bros Coffee, 1960   ▶▶ Del Monte, 196.

's high noon in the high Sierras. Time for everyone to . . .

...head for the Hills

Squaw Valley 1960! Host to all the world for the VIII Olympic
Winter Games. When it's time for coffee, here
or anywhere, it's time for Hills Bros.—the coffee chosen
to be served exclusively at the Winter Olympics.

Campbell's Soup, 1968

▶ Libby's, 19

cher in **NATURAL**
corn cream!

ust good eating . . . *superb* eating, that's Libby's Cream Style Corn.
edigreed . . . bred to produce plump, juicy kernels; then knowingly
ed to start the flow of that rich natural corn cream. The flavor, the
re are your tests that Libby's is the superior brand.

nd Wiener Roast—In baking dish, stir 2 tbsp. prepared mustard into 2 #303 cans
s Cream Style Corn. Add 8 wieners, gashed and stuffed with sharp cheese. Dot
ith butter and bake in mod. oven 20 min. *Libby, McNeill & Libby, Chicago 4, Ill.*

Libby's **cream·style corn**

And the winner is...

You Might Disappear
If dieting wasn't tough enough, the prospect of digging into a puddle of pink liquid instead of a substantial meal was about as appealing as chowing down on a bottle of Pepto Bismol instead of a steak.

Fasten bis zum bitteren Ende
Als ob Abnehmen an sich nicht schlimm genug wäre! Die Aussicht auf dieses rosa Gebräu anstelle einer ordentlichen Mahlzeit ist genauso verlockend wie die, anstatt eines Steaks eine ganze Flasche Magen-Darm-Medizin serviert zu bekommen.

Vous pourriez disparaître
Faire un régime c'est dur, mais la perspective de touiller dans une mare de liquide rose au lieu de prendre un repas substantiel était à peu près aussi excitante qu'avaler du bismuth au lieu de manger un steak.

Para desaparecer...
Por si hacer dieta no fuera ya bastante duro, la perspectiva de devorar un charco de líquido rosa, en lugar de un apetitoso plato de comida, resultaba tan atractiva como tomarse un litro de jarabe en lugar de un bistec.

あなたの姿が消えてなくなってしまうかも
ダイエットするだけでもつらいというのに、ちゃんとした食事の代わりにピンク色をした水たまり状のものにかぶりつくという考えは、ステーキの代わりにピンクの液状胃薬ペプトビスモルを食すのと同じぐらい魅惑的なものだったに違いない。

Drink a can of Metrecal® and you've had the nutrition of steak, potatoes, peas and carrots. But not the calories. Metrecal has only 225.

(And it comes in 14 different flavors—every one right out of an ice cream parlor.)

Metrecal for lunch and some common sense at other meals will help keep your weight right where you want it.

Two Metrecal meals a day (lunch and dinner), and you can lose weight steadily.

As for 3 a day, talk it over with your doctor first. You might disappear.

The Metrecal /teak.

About this picture: Our photographer said,"S Metrecal's a comp meal, let's shoo like one."

Metrecal, 1969

Surfline® photo courtesy of Wall Tube & Metal Products

Abominable Snowflakes

Snow can hurt. It ruins some outdoor furniture. But not this furniture. It's made with nickel stainless steel. It resists corrosion. Won't pit or roughen, stays gleaming, feels solid. Where does the nickel come in? Nickel is a unique metal that's rarely used alone. It's added to various metals to make them tougher, make them work better in all kinds of products. Remember, you get more out of anything that has nickel in it.

NICKEL STAINLESS STEEL
Enduring elegance. Won't scratch, pit, or whiten.
Nickel. Its contribution: **QUALITY**

International Nickel
New York, N.Y. 10005

A beautifully simple side chair of extraordinary comfort by Richard Schultz, of the Knoll Design and Development Unit.

Scaled to suit dining, meeting or lounge areas, it combines the softness of upholstery with an easily maintained plastic shell.

Base of aluminum or permanently fused finish.   Also available in a stackable version.

Just one of hundreds of Knoll furniture designs and textiles, designed for locations where beauty must be practical too.

The Knoll Planning Unit is available to plan and design complete interiors. May we send you an illustrated brochure?

KNOLL ASSOCIATES, INC., 320 PARK AVENUE, NEW YORK 22, N.Y.

Knoll Associates, 1963   ▶ *Congoleum-Nairn Flooring, 1960*

18 disks of foam rubber neatly arranged on
steel shafts support you comfortably on this
Marshmallow Loveseat by George Nelson.

Herman Miller
Furniture Co.
Los Angeles, Cal.

Herman Miller, 1960

▶ *Goodfoam Chairs, 1961*

Can be hung on wall or placed on a cabinet to suit your height. Available in 40-inch width (above) . . . or 30-inch Debutante model.

Everything's where it should be on the exclusive

Tappan 'Fabulous 400'

Gold Star Award gas range. The finest gas range built.

Gas or electric built-ins look alike. Wide choice of colors.

For 80 years, Tappan has been making ranges to suit the very special needs of every family. Today Tappan ranges offer more conveniences and more value than ever before. How proud you'll be of your new Gold Ribbon Tappan.

The Tappan Company, Mansfield, Ohio
Tappan-Gurney Limited, Montreal

Frigidaire, 1965 ◄ Tappan, 1961

And the winner is...

A Wonderful Feeling to Live with

With its nuclear family intact it was still possible for advertisers in the early sixties to sell the idea of a perfect world where climatic troubles were eliminated by "flameless electric comfort conditioning". Within a few years this bucolic tableau would be the victim of societal meltdown as divorce and electric rates began to soar and advertisers began to approach their product with more realistic portrayals.

Ein wunderbares Wohngefühl

Mit unerschüttertem Glauben an Familie und Atomkraft ließ es sich leicht für eine schöne neue Welt werben, in der Klimakatastrophen dank „elektrischer Komfort-Klimaanlagen ohne Verbrennung" nicht vorkamen. Doch innerhalb weniger Jahre fiel die Idylle der Realität zum Opfer, denn die Stromtarife schnellten ebenso hoch wie die Scheidungsraten – nun musste die Werbung zu realistischeren Bildern greifen.

Comme il est doux de vivre avec elle

Au début des années 60, la famille intacte permettait encore aux publicitaires de vendre l'idée d'un monde parfait où les troubles climatiques sont éliminés par un « confort électrique sans flamme ». Et puis, en l'espace de quelques années ce tableau bucolique se détériora, le nombre de divorces et de tarifs électriques se mit à augmenter et les publicitaires durent ajuster leurs produits aux réalités ambiantes.

Una sensación maravillosa

Con el núcleo familiar intacto, a principios de los años sesenta los publicistas aún podían vender la idea de un mundo perfecto donde las adversidades climáticas podían eliminarse con «estufas eléctricas sin llama». Transcurridos algunos años, este cuadro bucólico cayó víctima de una sociedad en la que el índice de divorcios y el precio de la electricidad se dispararon simultáneamente, lo cual llevó a los anunciantes a presentar sus productos con un enfoque más realista.

共に暮らすことで素晴らしい気分が味わえる

60年代初頭、核家族制度が無傷のままだったこの時代はまだ、広告主たちが、「火を使わない快適電気冷暖房装置」によって気候上の問題を排除した完璧な世界、などという発想を売り込むことが可能だった。この牧歌的なイラストは、ものの数年のうちに、社会崩壊の犠牲となって消えてゆくだろう。離婚率と電気料金が高騰し、広告主が商品を売るにあたってより現実的なアプローチを選択するがゆえに。

What a wonderful feeling to live with flameless electric comfort conditioning

Turn the page to see 15 special benefits you can enjoy in any home, old or new!

The end of
the plain plane,
explained.

It's obvious that our airplanes look—well—
different than other airplanes.

Not so obvious, perhaps, is why we made them
look different.

You see, all airplanes look pretty much the
same. And it was this monotonous *sameness* that
we were trying to get away from.

(Oooooh, how those 3-hour plane rides can
bore you. Especially if you're a guy who travels
for his living.)

Painting our airplanes different colors was a
step in the other direction.

We also changed the fabrics on the seats, the
uniforms our hostesses wear, our passenger lou

Braniff, 1966

ur food service.
  The list goes on and on.
  In fact, we've made 17,543 changes in our airline
far. (This includes the small ones, like the
ther satisfying change we made in the package that
olds the sugar for your coffee.)
  Since no other airline has ever gone to so much

trouble before, you may still not understand
why *we* did.
  But even if you can't understand it, you can relax
and enjoy it.

Braniff International
United States Mexico South America

Convair's 880, the only American-built jet airliner with **all first-class seating**, brings you an entirely new travel concept in speed, splendor and spectacular performance! With the **880** you're flying on the fastest, newest and most advanced jet passenger plane in the world!

CONVAIR

A DIVISION OF **GENERAL DYNAMICS CORPORATION**

First to offer Convair 880 or 600 service will be TWA, DELTA, REAL-AEROVIAS (Brazil), SWISSAIR, S.A.S., AMERICAN, C.A.T. (Formosa), AVENSA (Venezuela), JAL (Japan)

SHERATON
AT THE HEART OF WAIKIKI

THE FOUR HOTELS THAT MADE WAIKIKI FAMOUS

ROYAL HAWAIIAN
Pleasure...18-acres big beside the sparkling Pacific!

PRINCESS KAIULANI
Orchid swimming pool for Polynesian splash parties!

MOANA AND SURFRIDER
Glamorous twosome, side by side, to double your fun!

STAY AT ONE—PLAY AT ALL FOUR

Sheraton's where the fun is! Just 4½ jet-hours from the mainland. 70° surf-and-sun days, Fun Festival brighten every Diamond Head night, feasts every meal, service every moment. Family plan: children s adult's accommodations free. For easy reservations, just call your travel agent or your nearest Sheraton H **Open Dec. 1: Sheraton-Maui, dazzling resort hotel on magnificent Kaanapali Beach · Maui, Hav**

Sheraton shares are listed on the New York Stock Exchange.   *Diners' Club card honored for all hotel ser*

OPENS APRIL 21

SEATTLE WORLD'S FAIR 1962

The curtain's going up on America's first World's Fair in two decades. For 180 days, millions will step beyond the boundaries of today's world for a way-ahead look into another age. See for yourself how the family of tomorrow will live, work and play in the most spectacular, breathtaking forecast science ever made. Preview out-of-this-world concepts of living in space . . . on the ground . . . under the sea! Match it all with the best of our world today—its art, its entertainment, its varied culture—coming to life before your eyes in a sparkling $80 million showcase of pleasure and delight!

A FLOATING CITY OF TOMORROW! A rotating "bubbleator" in Washington State's gigantic Coliseum elevates 100 persons at a time to a fascinating portrayal of life's wonders in the year 2000.

MILE-A-MINUTE MONORAIL! The thrilling ride of a lifetime on the noiseless monorail gliding above busy downtown Seattle streets to its World's Fair terminal . . . 10,000 passengers hourly!

A RESTAURANT THAT REVOLVES IN THE SKY! 600 feet up, the lacy fingers of the Space Needle reach toward the clouds, crowned by an observation deck, dining room, and a soaring jet of flame!

ROCKET RIDE TO MARS! Leave the world behind as you take a just-pretend journey 2 billion light years into space in the Boeing Company's Spacearium at the breath-taking U. S. Science Pavilion.

WORLD'S GREATEST STARS! Stravinsky, The Old Vic, Count Basie: A continuous parade of leading entertainers performs for you in the opulent Opera House, the Playhouse, the Arena and the Stadium.

SHOW STREET! Gorgeous girls take you behind the scenes as part of the act at "Backstage, U. S. A." It's one of the Fair's many glamorous nighteries.

GAY, EXOTIC BOULEVARDS OF THE WORLD! A potpourri of scents, sounds, and tastes from 35 foreign nations. Trees and fountains line the beautifully landscaped malls and plazas.

IT'S A HUGE, GLAMOROUS, EXCITING SHOW set in one of the world's most beautiful modern cities. See it all, starting April 21, for 180 unforgettable days and nights! It's the blazing, amazing adventure of a lifetime . . . the world's salute to a new age!

PACIFIC NORTHWEST OPENS ITS DOORS! A Western welcome and room for all awaits you. For reservations in Washington, Oregon and British Columbia as you travel to and from the Fair—and for your Seattle stay—write Expo-Lodging Service, Inc., Seattle 9, Wash. Confirmed reservations possible in Seattle through Expo-Lodging in hotels, motels, apartment-hotels and approved private homes.

EVERY PLACE YOU WANT TO GO—all the things you want to see . . . are just hours away from the big Seattle show. Take time to see it all. You'll love every minute of it!

Washington
*is a Wonder-FULL State
. . . See it ALL while
you're here!*

Dept. B, SEATTLE WORLD'S FAIR, SEATTLE 9, WASHINGTON
Please send me the following:
Further information about Seattle World's Fair and a Washington State vacation ☐
Further information about World's Fair housing accommodations ☐

Name ....

Address ....

City .... State ....
(PLEASE PRINT CLEARLY)   C-31-L-3

WASHINGTON STATE DEPARTMENT OF COMMERCE AND ECONOMIC DEVELOPMENT, Albert D. Rosellini, Governor

And the winner is...

Something very Interesting on the Aisle
Ahh! Those Go Go years of air travel. If mini-skirted stewardesses and the vague hint of sex and booze weren't enough to get you on aboard, how about prices that competed with a full tank of gas?

Alles Gute kommt von oben
Ach, ferne Tage unbeschwerten Fliegens! Wem damals die Stewardessen im Minirock und die vage Aura von Sexappeal und Hochprozentigem nicht reichten, den überzeugte bestimmt der Preis – ein Flug kostete kaum mehr als eine Tankfüllung.

Des choses très intéressantes dans le couloir
Ah! Ces années où on s'envoyait en l'air. Si les hôtesses en minijupes et leur vague promesse de délices au-dessus des nuages ne suffisaient pas à vous attirer à bord, peut-être étiez-vous sensible aux tarifs qui peuvent entrer en compétition avec le prix d'un réservoir plein d'essence.

Un pasillo de sensaciones
¡Ah, aquellos maravillosos años! ¿Qué podría ser mejor que volar en la década de los sesenta? Por si las azafatas yeyé en minifalda y la insinuación de la posibilidad de disfrutar de sexo y alcohol no fueran suficientes para invitar al público a subir a bordo, ¿quién podría resistirse a surcar los cielos por lo mismo que le costaría llenar el depósito de su automóvil de gasolina?

通路では、かなり面白いことがあるかも
ああ! 空の旅がイケイケだった古きよき時代。もしも、当機にご搭乗いただくにあたって、ミニスカートのスチュワーデスと、ほのかに暗示されたセックスと酒の匂いでもご満足いただけないようなら、満タンのガソリンと変わらない低料金はいかがですか?

PSA AISLE SEATS $13.50*

WHILE THEY LAST

On other airlines everybody wants the window seats. On PSA they prefer the aisle view. Guess why? More new jets and 900 flights a week connecting Northern and Southern California. Call PSA or your travel agent for something very interesting on the aisle.

*L.A.-San Francisco 727 Super Jets

PSA gives you a lift

spy novels, Le Carré himself has ignored the libidinous and gone directly to the problem of the confused identities of bumbling anti-heroes. *A Small Town in Germany* is more a skillful novel of political intrigue than a spy story, but Le Carré's aim is still the same.

The scene is the "recent future" in Bonn, a time of Britain's critical attempt to negotiate her way into the Common Market. Leo Harting, a minor official in the British embassy, has disappeared with secret files that could ruin the negotiations. Alan Turner, a counterespionage agent reminiscent of the half-burnt-out, seedy Alec Leamas of *The Spy Who Came In from the Cold*, has been sent from London to find Harting and recapture the missing documents. So far, a familiar situation. But Turner's main antagonists are not foreign spies; they are the British embassy officials themselves—a caste-conscious, emotionally aborted, washed-out crew of professional liars.

Counterpunching. Le Carré has picked up the destructive intramural rivalries of espionage in *The Looking Glass War* and moved them into the illusion-fed machinations of the diplomatic life. The search, ultimately, is not only for Leo Harting but for clues to the personal identity that Harting managed to retain while in the service of depersonalizing ideological powers. As it turns out, both Harting and Turner have been counterpunching with a diplomatic shadow world; they are both, says Turner, "looking for something that isn't there." Le Carré, playing off the man of ideals against men of duplicity, touches once again on the theme that has elevated him above the average suspense novelist. The philosophical conclusion he arrives at is basically the same that he found for Leamas. Speaking to another character, Turner says of Harting:

"For you and me there are always a dozen good reasons for doing nothing. Leo's made the other way around. In Leo's book there's only one reason for doing something: because he must. Because he feels."

It is this awareness that reveals Le Carré as the Sartre of diplomatic and espionage literature. His protagonists stumble through the subterranean maze of contemporary crises in search of a sudden illuminating truth, such as the one that strikes Turner as he unravels the cause of Harting's betrayal. Hatred was not Harting's motive; instead, it was a need to defy the aimlessness and indifference of diplomatic life. "He'd escaped from lethargy. That's the point, isn't it: the opposite of love isn't hate. It's lethargy. Nothingness."

Le Carré tells about that journey through nothingness with the same clean, tough style that he mastered in his earlier works—a lucid grasp on the physical and emotional landscapes that allows him the occasional power of poetic insight.

PSA Airlines, 1968

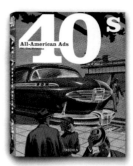

All-American Ads of the 40s
W.R. Wilkerson III, Ed. Jim
Heimann / Flexi-cover, 768 pp. /
€ 29.99 / $ 39.99 / £ 19.99 /
¥ 5.900

All-American Ads of the 50s
Ed. Jim Heimann / Flexi-cover,
928 pp. / € 29.99 / $ 39.99 /
£ 19.99 / ¥ 5.900

All-American Ads of the 60s
Steven Heller, Ed. Jim Heimann /
Flexi-cover, 960 pp. / € 29.99 /
$ 39.99 / £ 19.99 / ¥ 5.900

"The ads do more than advertise products – they provide a record of American everyday life of a bygone era in a way that nothing else can." —*Associated Press*, USA

"Buy them all and add some pleasure to your life."

African Style
Ed. Angelika Taschen

Alchemy & Mysticism
Alexander Roob

All-American Ads 40ˢ
Ed. Jim Heimann

All-American Ads 50ˢ
Ed. Jim Heimann

All-American Ads 60ˢ
Ed. Jim Heimann

Angels
Gilles Néret

Architecture Now!
Ed. Philip Jodidio

Art Now
Eds. Burkhard Riemschneider,
Uta Grosenick

Atget's Paris
Ed. Hans Christian Adam

Berlin Style
Ed. Angelika Taschen

Chairs
Charlotte & Peter Fiell

Christmas
Steven Heller

Design of the 20ᵗʰ Century
Charlotte & Peter Fiell

Design for the 21ˢᵗ Century
Charlotte & Peter Fiell

Devils
Gilles Néret

Digital Beauties
Ed. Julius Wiedemann

Robert Doisneau
Ed. Jean-Claude Gautrand

East German Design
Ralf Ulrich / Photos: Ernst
Hedler

Egypt Style
Ed. Angelika Taschen

M.C. Escher

Fashion
Ed. The Kyoto Costume
Institute

HR Giger
HR Giger

Grand Tour
Harry Seidler,
Ed. Peter Gössel

Graphic Design
Ed. Charlotte & Peter Fiell

Greece Style
Ed. Angelika Taschen

Halloween Graphics
Steven Heller

Havana Style
Ed. Angelika Taschen

Homo Art
Gilles Néret

Hot Rods
Ed. Coco Shinomiya

Hula
Ed. Jim Heimann

Indian Style
Ed. Angelika Taschen

India Bazaar
Samantha Harrison,
Bari Kumar

Industrial Design
Charlotte & Peter Fiell

Japanese Beauties
Ed. Alex Gross

Krazy Kids' Food
Eds. Steve Roden,
Dan Goodsell

Las Vegas
Ed. Jim Heimann

London Style
Ed. Angelika Taschen

Mexicana
Ed. Jim Heimann

Mexico Style
Ed. Angelika Taschen

Morocco Style
Ed. Angelika Taschen

**Extra/Ordinary Objects,
Vol. I**
Ed. Colors Magazine

**Extra/Ordinary Objects,
Vol. II**
Ed. Colors Magazine

Paris Style
Ed. Angelika Taschen

Penguin
Frans Lanting

20ᵗʰ Century Photography
Museum Ludwig Cologne

Pin-Ups
Ed. Burkhard Riemschneider

Photo Icons I
Hans-Michael Koetzle

Photo Icons II
Hans-Michael Koetzle

Pierre et Gilles
Eric Troncy

Provence Style
Ed. Angelika Taschen

Pussycats
Gilles Néret

Safari Style
Ed. Angelika Taschen

Seaside Style
Ed. Angelika Taschen

Albertus Seba. Butterflies
Irmgard Müsch

**Albertus Seba. Shells &
Corals**
Irmgard Müsch

South African Style
Ed. Angelika Taschen

Starck
Ed Mae Cooper, Pierre Doze,
Elisabeth Laville

Surfing
Ed. Jim Heimann

Sweden Style
Ed. Angelika Taschen

Sydney Style
Ed. Angelika Taschen

Tattoos
Ed. Henk Schiffmacher

Tiffany
Jacob Baal-Teshuva

Tiki Style
Sven Kirsten

Tuscany Style
Ed. Angelika Taschen

Web Design: Best Studios
Ed. Julius Wiedemann

Women Artists
in the 20ᵗʰ and 21ˢᵗ Century
Ed. Uta Grosenick

★
ICONS